UNDERSTANDING
MEANING
AND
PURPOSE
OF ROCK ART

D. Russel Micnhimer

UNDERSTANDING MEANING AND PURPOSE OF ROCK ART

Pendulum Press

ISBN 978-09740105-8-8

First edition January 2012

0 9 8 7 6 5 4 3 2 1

COVER: LeeAnn Johnston photograph
         The author
         Long Lake, Oregon
         Design by Charlie Comstock

Printed in USA

Dedication

**This book is lovingly dedicated
to
LeeAnn Johnston
with thanks for her ongoing love,
inspiration and companionship.**

Special thanks to Frank Crosser and Bob Andrews
for their editorial advice and proofreading and to
Charlie Comstock for designing and laying out the
cover. My gratitude to my aunt, Marilyn
Henderson, for inspiration and mentoring. Any
errors remain the sole responsibility of the author.

"I think and think for months and years, ninety-nine times, the conclusion is false. The hundredth time I am right."
Albert Einstein

TABLE OF CONTENTS

All photographs are taken by the author except where
otherwise noted and are copyright by the author.
Most are from sites in western North America. Some
images may be slightly distorted due to formatting.
They are unannotated so readers may draw their own
conclusions as to meaning and purpose.

FORWORD

As an avocational archaeologist, I have been aware of the existence of rock art for most of my life. There were a couple of sites near where I grew up in Eastern Oregon and those were visited with family, especially when there was company to whom we were showing the sights. For the past two decades I have been increasingly focused on the exploration and recording of rock art, both in Oregon and the other western states. I've visited hundreds of sites in person and become acquainted with many others throughout the world via existing literature and the Internet. This account is driven by my love of inquiry and a solid belief that, by asking the right questions, the right answers may be obtained. Many answers that are not correct are also discovered along the way, these too have value. They make us think. And to use an analogy from the field of sales, each "no" gets us that much closer to the next "yes."

To arrive at an understanding of the meaning and purpose of rock art there are a number of ways in which I feel the subject needs to be approached. These questions that need to be explored are not unique to this discussion but are a convenient way of organizing our inquiry. Who made rock art? When

7

was it made? How was it made? What was made?
And finally, why was it made?

Many sources have attempted to answer many of
these questions, often in very regionally specific
ways. These answers tend to become more clear and
comprehensive as the volume of research increases
and as more technological tools become available.
The answer to the question, why was rock art made,
however,   in   my   opinion,   has   not   been
comprehensively addressed in a single work. It is my
goal with this writing to change that. This is not to
say that there are not already some ideas about what
rock art means—there are. And many of them no
doubt have validity. It is not my intention to take
issue with those ideas. Rather, I have chosen to
systematically examine as many factors as I can
think of that seem to have some bearing on what the
meaning and purpose of rock art is. If you bought
this book expecting to find a clear and simple answer
to the question, what is the meaning and purpose of
rock art, I suggest you return it now for your money
back. I will not be able to give you a definitive
answer. But it is my hope, that by reading this, you
will be much closer to arriving at an answer yourself.
And it is my fervent hope that with enough individual
minds applied to the question, at some point in the
future, more definitive answers will be revealed. By
its nature though, the answer will always require the

plural—what are the "MEANINGS and PURPOSES" of rock art.

It will be obvious quite early on that my writing style is somewhat colloquial. This may hinder some more educated readers' enjoyment but I hope it will not obscure the ideas I wish to convey. Obviously this is not a scientifically prepared paper so sources will seldom be cited. A subject this broad draws information from many sources, from both inside and outside the discipline. I by no means claim that all the ideas herein are my own, although I do accept sole responsibility for any inaccuracies in interpretations of other's ideas. Since this is not a scientific treatise, there are no footnotes nor a list of source material. Most of the material studied was accessed before the idea of this book was conceived.

Many of the ideas herein are illustrated by hypothetical examples. And, while there may be certain inherent dangers in using such to support particular notions, it is hoped that the hypotheticals are at least within the realm of reason. Every attempt has been made to purify such examples by ridding them, to the fullest extent possible, of my cultural biases. Occasionally I indulge in unbridled speculation. For that I offer no apologies. As a poet, that is part of my nature, and I can hope that by sharing in this manner it may lead others' imaginations toward increased understanding. One way in which understanding grows is by analogy. It is by examining all possibilities, no matter how far afield, and from them extracting reasonable hypothesis that can be analyzed with scientific methods, that will lead, in the long run, to higher understandings in the approach to truth.

It is my main premise that no single theory or explanation about why petroicons were created will suffice to reveal the variety of their meaning. (I use the term "petroicon" in an attempt to divest the description of any bias the term "art" may imply. In its original form the Greek word *icon* meant an image, a figure or a likeness; and *petra* meant rock. In using that term, I am at odds with many of my colleagues; be that as it may, I will on occasion employ it.) A myopic approach that disregards any interpretation that doesn't fit a premise, is one that I find counter productive and an attitude I can ill afford if this effort is to succeed. In some cases, it is only by broadening current definitional restraints that existing paradigms may be changed. I offer this work as a point of beginning, a comprehensive survey of factors I believe must be necessarily taken into consideration if we are ever to answer the fundamental question—what are the meanings and purposes of rock art?

Because we can seldom, if ever, be in direct contact with the minds of those who created these markings on stones, most conclusions must contain an element of speculation. As the time of their creation regresses, the likelihood that we can ever know with certainty the answers to the fundamental question recedes as well. Although the converse may be argued, as this book does, that the more we study the evidence, the closer we can approach the knowing of their true meaning. A balanced approach keeps this paradox in mind.

Rock art research is yet in its infancy as part of the discipline of archaeology.   With the enormous number of rock art sites that occur world wide-- conservatively estimated at more than half a million —the problem of establishing meaning and purpose in any universal sense is probably insurmountable. Rock art in different geographic locations and different temporal eras had different meanings and purposes. But by examining the fundamentals of particular cases, certain verities may be discovered that have broad applications. With the promulgation of those truths, the progress of research can be furthered.

Attitudes toward the meaning of rock art are diverse. They range from I don't care, why should I care, it's none of my business, we can never know, we are not supposed to know, it is of no use to conjecture, only those who made it can know, only the descendants of those who made it can know, we can know if we count every image, if we measure every image, if we name every image, if we record how often each image occurs, to it has no meaning at all, every interpretation is just a guess, this is bad, I must destroy it, this is bad, I must replace it with my own, to someone made some marks here, I will too.

My attitude may be summed up this way. Even within the society whose members created these markings on stones, their meaning may not have been universally understood. Only the makers themselves may have known why they made them. They may have passed their understanding on to only a selected few in the group. Couple this with the frequently long periods of time over which they were produced and the question of meaning and becomes further complicated and even less transparent. Perhaps we are destined to be able to only "gaze and guess," but it is my hope that after reading this book, those guesses can at least be based on as many relevant factors as possible.

Tranquility Base, Prineville, Oregon

October 14, 2011

INTRODUCTION

Most readers are familiar with the wide variety of rock art that exists throughout the world. Where ever and when ever human kind has visited and there are stone surfaces, marks have been made. Some of those marks may have been left incidentally; scrapes and grooves as a result of the use of levers, edge sharpening and employment of other tools such as plows, certainly exist and are deserving of study in their own right. We may assume that, aside from being artifacts of usage, they have little or no further significance.

That the remainder of the marks, which I shall sometimes refer to as petroicons, had some meaning is the *a priori* assumption that underlies this book. It may of course be argued that some of it is meaningless idle doodling or unintentioned graffiti. As we shall see, even if that was its *raison d' etre,* it was created with purpose and therefore, meaning. For our intentions here, we shall consider any rock art that does not include expressions of language or its prototypes. Some might argue that rock art is "thought writing." Whether we agree with that definition or not, it does stand to reason that there is a continuum between the first very primitive marks on stone through the very complex depictions of ideas presented on stone media in the round, i.e. sculpture. That is a topic outside the realm of this book.

Common sense and study strongly suggest that, at some time, past, present and/or future, rock art is meaningful and had a purpose for being made. To explore what that meaning may be, we must view it in light of several questions that are frequently asked during such investigations. As with any discussion of a complex subject there are overlapping areas and of course, all facets are ultimately interlinked and each nodule of knowledge adds to the overall understanding. We must be extremely careful during this process in what we project from our modern mindset onto the mindset of those who may have produced rock art in the past. It is the nature of understanding that many meanings change over time as further information becomes available.

The questions we must address to further our understanding are the following:

Who made it? What was their sex? Age? Relationship to people for whom it was intended—husband, wife, lover, child, parent, no relation, friend, acquaintance, stranger, enemy? What was their social position—peer, priest, shaman, leader, cartographer? Were they near sighted, far sighted, blind in one eye, blind, dyslexic or did they have cataracts? Does it reflect the interior dreams, visions and thoughts of the maker? Does it address the creator's interpretation of world view or their interpretation of the mechanisms where by the world works? How does the process of abstracting symbols from reality actually work; how is that information internalized and then expressed? What changes does the information undergo during the various stages of the process?

Where was it made? For its full meaning to be comprehended it must be placed in context both temporally and culturally. Was the culture a hunter/gatherer society, rural/agrarian or sedentary/urban? What is the context in which we find it? Was it in living areas? Slightly outside them? Isolated? Hidden? Public? Near a well traveled or seldom traveled path? Was it near food or other resources? How does it reflect the relationship of the creator with the exterior natural world around them?

How was it made? Were layers made at the same time? Were superimpositions meant to interact with the images made previously at the same panel? Were they meant to negate them, modify them or supplement them? Was it painted or pecked? Was the method meaningful or simply a matter of expediency with the tools and materials available? Was it made with great care and attention to detail or in a seemingly haphazard fashion?

When was it made? Were they mnemonic devices used as aids in the locating of food or water resources by the same people at a future time or as aids for people in the future to locate the same commodities? Or as markers to indicate where caches of valuables were concealed for future use? How much, if any, cross generational meaning can we infer? Was it produced to communicate to others in the time immediately after its execution? Or for a purpose in the future of the lifetime of the maker? For followers later through the same territory? Or for future generations? Or for posterity?

What was made? Was it simply a copy of something in real life that had been actually observed by the creator? Was the something real? Or was it illusionary? Was it something the creator had been told about? Was it something the creator imagined or dreamed about? Or experienced while in an altered state due to sickness, plant ingestion or both? What was the motivation? What was the inspiration? Was it new or copied from somewhere? What were the variables involved in any particular image? Was just the sense of sight being evoked or were other senses trying to be engaged such as hearing for music, fragrance such as a drawing of a flower, touch as in texture of fur or vegetable matter, or the mind with a calendar? Were single simple ideas being illustrated? Or more complex ideas using numerous and/or compound images? Was the image representational, symbolic, random or deliberate, or a combination of these?

Why was it made? We must take into consideration its image, its intended audience, its timing and its intent. Were the marks made as visual symbols to convey information, to evoke aesthetic feelings or were they simply by products of activities such as noise producing percussion or the generation of stone powder for other uses such as pigments or medicinal purposes? Or did the empty space left behind once a bowl or a talisman had been created from a rock have significance? Can we assume that pre-linguist visual markings may have a direct correspondence with the same concerns that lingual (alphabets, etc.) did later? Did some of them represent proto-writing or imitations of sign language? Was their function to represent identity, counting, mapping or territorial boundaries?

Was there a hierarchy of meaning—from decorative, to mundane, from pornographic to highly spiritual? How reliable is ethnographic interpretation; does it get more suspect the farther back it tries to reach in time? Are there cases where meaning can be deduced through self referencing iconology?

All of these ideas complicate considerably what on first hearing seems like a simple question—what does it mean?   By discovering a combination of the inspiration and the skill of execution, perhaps the maker of the marks' true intent may be revealed. Perhaps only by understanding the objective of the original producer, a true understanding of meaning may be developed. It is imperative that we keep in mind there is not a single explanation that may be applied universally and further that certain long standing ideas may be challenged by reexamination. One need only cite the stumbling stones of a series of wrong conclusions that were accepted as starting points and prevented the translation of Mayan glyphs for several decades, to validate the importance of applying a fresh, new and comprehensive approach to the challenge. It is quite unlikely there will ever be discovered   a source analogous   to the "Rosetta Stone" that might greatly reduce the effort required for the task. Some widely accepted ideas such as the causes and nature of shamanistic visions, need to be more thoroughly explored and tested before they are accepted as facts. Some terms, in any discipline, tend to become catch all repositories for information that is not understood or sufficiently observed to fit well else where in the paradigm. This tends to dilute the meaning of the term so it has little true usefulness for furthering understanding.

I am optimistic that, with the establishment of the framework of lenses offered here, through which any particular instance of petroiconology may be examined, deeper understandings of why and for what purposes these marks were made on stone may be garnered.

20

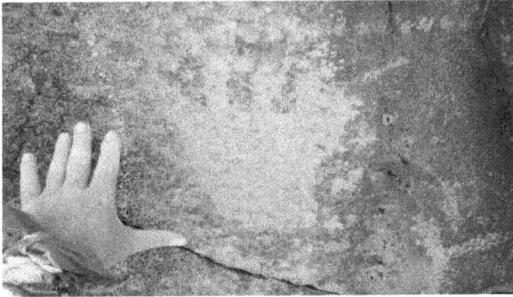

21

22

CHAPTER ONE

WHO MADE ROCK ART? FOR WHOM WAS IT MADE?

We begin with the most fundamental of questions. Who made rock art?

The ethnographic record suggests that in many cases, rock art was made by people who lived before historical memories. Its production is variously attributed to supernatural entities, mythological figures or by spirits or their helpers. These explanatory traditions reach far back in time in some cases, from which we can conclude that even when some were being made, their makers may have wanted to preserve a sense of mystery about their origins. There are some places in the world such as Australia where rock art is still being made and a continuity of sorts between the current makers and the previous is part of the tradition. For the most part though, the memory of who the makers were has faded with their corporeality and even ethnic groups that still occupy the land where rock art is found, are at a loss to supply any but vague identifications.

While there may have been occasions when the process of making rock art was undertaken by more than one person at the same place at the same time, it is safe assumption that in most cases at least, each element, even on collaborative panels, is the product of a single maker.

This assumption allows us to make the basic identity of the maker definable.

It was biologically either a male or a female.

They were of a particular age when they made the glyph.

They were in a particular state of mental and physical health.

They had a particular status and role in the family, group and society.

There was a reason and/or inspiration for the production.

There was an intended audience for the image (although, in some cases that audience may have been only the maker them self.)

Whether male or female, there are shared commonalities.   If we assume some degree of individuality, then we may assume that each person had an appellation. A name by which they were referred. And there may in fact have been many names referring to a single individual just as today we have formal legal names, first, middle and family names, nicknames, pet names, and generic names. "Fatty," "Skinny", "Sweetheart", "Dear", diminutive forms, Joe for Joseph; modified, Steverino for Steven; intentionally mispronounced, "DeeDee" for Deann. There are names and nick names within groups both large and small. In high school, Geeks and Jocks; as a function of profession, "Doc" for Doctor; in the world at large The People and The Enemy; Czechoslovakians and Bohunks and Mexicans and Beaners. These are but a few examples of "names" by which individuals may be known and certainly more than one may apply to any given individual.

Additionally, as it is today, it may be assumed that multiple individuals may have shared the same name, due to its widespread usage, such as "son" or "sen" being added to surnames to mean "son of" as in some Nordic traditions, or simply as a popular name due to a famous figure such as "Jesus" or "Maria" among many Hispanic populations or as a faddish style such as "Jordan" or "Cheyenne" for girls in the late twentieth century.

If we may extrapolate from today, it seems an innate urge once we learn that we may make marks that stand for our name, we want to repeat the making of those marks. Small kids crayon their names on walls, punk kids tag walls with graffiti names, soldiers leave "Kilroy was here" on fences. They become a testament to our existence. Might this not have been so even before the codification of spoken language into written symbols?

Male or female, it seems to be ingrained in our nature to leave a mark that says, "I was here."

Now let us examine the age factor. We may generalize and say that up to a certain point, say puberty, there are probably not many marks made that are gender distinctive. In European caves, marks have been found that appear to have resulted from very young children wiping their fingers on the surface. Assigning significance to such marks seems ludicrous, but there are those who argue that even very small, seemingly insignificant marks, may have been made with intention and hence meaning by adults. It is probably a safe assumption that in some cases where children observed adults "drawing" on walls they may have sought to imitate their elders. There are examples around the world of very tiny hand and foot prints in rock art traditions, although in all likelihood, those were made by adults, not by children, as children as small as depicted would not have had the skills to have done so . As children grew older, influences from outside the immediate family increased. Visual examples such as circles or dots, imparted by peers, older siblings or playmates, societal traditions and the general increase in awareness of surroundings added to the body of imagery that may have sought expression in suitable environments outside the young minds.

With the onset of puberty and its attendant ritualized social recognitions, gender began to play an increasingly larger role in the types of visual symbology that was recorded on stone.

For females of course, the onset of menses marked a distinct milestone in the aging process. Nearly every society had various means of acknowledging this event, many of which entailed some form of isolation and revelation by elder women about the nature of the transition. In many cases, rituals were involved which required the transitioning young woman to make note of the occasion by making marks on stone. Some elder teachers may have used existing marks, sometimes by refreshing or reinforcing them, and have made new ones, for purposes of instructing the emergent adults about proper rituals and behavioral processes, both physical and mental, associated with their coming of age.

While coming of age in males was not marked by such a distinctive event as menses in females, when the time came for a male to transition from a "boy" to a "man," there were also ritualized activities of initiation, some of which required the production of petroicons. The recognition of the right to use and methods of reproducing clan symbols may have been included in these activities. Symbol making as an aid to warrior and hunting prowess would have been promulgated by elders during this time.

The practice of spiritual vision quests, while more frequently part of male adolescent activity, was also practiced by females in some societies. Often these quests entailed harsh physical stresses such as fasting, running or climbing difficult courses and isolation for extended periods of time. During these quests, visions of spiritual assistance were sought, frequently in the form of animals or combinations of animals and other spirits. Records of evocation of these visitations or of the visions themselves were often made on stone at the site where the visions took place. Frequently these markings on stone were made in very inaccessible, hidden locations that only the participant had visited, as a means of sanctifying the experience. Such quests may have been repeated by some individuals well into adulthood. A similar behavior may have been undertaken at times of crisis in an individual's life when solitude was sought, perhaps to mourn a loss or as a "time out" for contemplation of life altering decisions. During such times glyphs may have been produced in commemoration or as a mental and emotional aid to deal with the crisis at hand.

Those of either gender who pursued what today we call "spiritual" matters, sometimes alone, but more frequently under more mature tutelage, became known as healers, medicine beings or shamans. Their rituals and practices often involved the use of markings on stones. Their "magical" and "healing" abilities were often a result of learning the healing properties of various plants and minerals.   The images such individuals made on stones may be initially thought of in two ways: as instrumental or symbolic.

Instrumental markings derived their meanings from the process of their creation. A mark made by a shaman demonstrating the striking of an enemy would serve as an example; perhaps by the mere touching of such marks their power could be imbued on the person touching them. In some cases certain scents or odors may have been incorporated into the glyph manufacture and by having the associated olfactory experience, the desired outcome would thought to have been facilitated. Such distinctive specialist members of a group may have discovered that the powdered form of certain stones was good for treatment of certain ailments, mineral deficiencies or conditions. In the process of extracting such powders marks such as cupules may have been left behind.   Marks such as these are frequently interpreted as part of the rock art record.

The meaning of symbolic marks would have been closely tied to magical practices. Magic may be classified in three ways, each of which would have had attendant forms of stone markings.

First, sympathetic magic. Simply put, if you wanted it to rain, you would sprinkle water as an imitation of the desired result or perhaps peck a series of dots on a rock as if rain were falling on it. If you wanted to attract game, you might draw a picture of the quarry, supplemented with those of weapons, depictions of strategies for hunting it or red drops representing the blood of a kill. Before going on a hunt, one might strike an image of the hunted animal repeatedly in the head or heart with arrows, or spears or another stone to reinforce the idea of killing it. Complimenting that you might depict the killed animal as a symbol of your thankfulness for its sacrifice in hopes of attracting others in the future.

Second, ritual magic. If you had determined, for instance, that a certain series of actions or activities was necessary to ensure a desired end, you might make notes of what those were and the desired sequence. This may have served as a mnemonic devise for repletion of the ritual or as a device for teaching the ritual to others. By way of example, a sequence of glyphs might depict a tilling of soil, a planting of seeds, sprouting of the plant, irrigation of the plant, maturation, harvesting, storing and saving seed for the next planting. If nets or stone drive blinds were to be used as an aid in the capture and slaughter of an animal, drawings depicting the arrangements of such devices and the arrangement of the animals within them may be depicted to help ensure success.

Third, talismanic magic. Certain images made on stone may have been perceived as affording protection of some sort. That imagery would have been affixed to a portable stone by means similar to marks on less mobile surfaces, and its power extended to those who kept it with them in a form such as an amulet or pendant. Many portable stones with such markings have been found throughout the world.

Although it may have varied less in less complicated times, each individual, male and female, would have had both a genealogical and biographical history just as they do today.

Genealogical records would have been important whether the society was matrilineal or patrilineal. What particular symbols may have been used to keep track of these generational lines is difficult to guess, although it may be assumed that the task could have been of equal importance to either sex. Perhaps clan or symbols that represented the group as well as "personal" names were modified to reflect relationships. Perhaps a generic image such as a ship may have been used to delineate a generation. Particularly when life spans were much shorter, such mnemonic devices would have significant value. Each individual would also have a number of familial relationships—son, daughter, parent, sibling, in-law, etc. There may have been occasions such as marriages or funerals where glyphs indicative of such relationships were used.

The biographic details of a person's life probably had values varying from individual to individual just as they do today. It is a safe assumption though that feats and accomplishments of extraordinary note were repeated in story and song and, at least on occasion, must have been the impetus for the making of markings on stone. Such occurrences could have happened at any time during a life.

That such experiences may have occurred to the group as a whole seems a given. Whether the occasion was a tragedy that effected many members, a extraordinary discovery, perhaps of a food resource, or a large scale migration, they would have been recorded in the most prevalent media available—markings on stone.

As people became of advanced age, they may have come to have known certain things that they wanted to pass along to younger generations. While certainly the oral tradition would have served this purpose most frequently, it is not unreasonable to believe that marks on stone may have been made by elders with the hope that lessons and knowledge they had gathered in a lifetime might be preserved.

Three things that varied throughout the years of a person's life might have influenced the making of glyphs—health, state of mind and "artistic" ability.

Although there may have been other health factors
that influenced the making of marks on stone, the one
that most obviously comes to mind is eyesight and
various degrees of visual acuity. While most people
probably had "20/20" vision, there would have been
portions of the populace that were either near or far
sighted. This would have influenced the way in
which they perceived reality around them and the
way in which they would have depicted it with their
markings. Due to accident or genetic birth defects
there were doubtlessly people who were blind and
who only had one eye. The blind may have made
tactile imprints on stone just as braille is created
today. While it would not have represented language
as braille does and the makers wouldn't have been
able to see it, it would still be visible to others.
Binocular   perception among single eyed people
would surely have effected and been reflected in their
representations. Just as today, a sharp bump to the
head may cause a person to "see stars," it may be that
some who experienced such insults to the brain tried
to reproduce those phosphenes in their markings on
the stones. Even today one may glance repeatedly
and briefly at a bright light such as a setting sun and
for sometime afterwards "see" an after image while
blinking the eyes. Physical mobility in its various
life stages would have an influence on where in the
landscape marks could be made.

Individual "artistic ability" would not only have varied from individual to individual but with degrees of practice and training. Some groups may have even had members whose function was designated as the "mark maker." Their abilities may have been learned from earlier practitioners and their skill level varied with their learning ability. Just as today, a child when first asked to draw a picture of himself or another person may produce a very rudimentary "stick" figure and later add details such as fingers and toes, this seems to have parallels in the rock art record. Stylistic conventions would have influenced the manner in which glyphs from the same tradition were made; those of course would have been adapted and modified by individual members of such groups.

The mental and emotional state of the makers would have significant influence on the outcome of their efforts. As mentioned before in relation to vision quest rites, physical stress from fatigue, fasting, isolation or other activities would have influences. "Normal" states may be differentiated from "supernatural states" modified by trances induced by dancing, drumming or by use of plants which altered brain chemistry. Such states are generally believed to have been experienced by "shamans." Much has been made by theoreticians about various drug induced stages as perception is altered causing the person who has ingested the substance to "see" universal designs. This occurs, although there is much yet to be learned before accepting the universality of such designs and accompanying theories.   That such imagery was depicted in markings on rocks though can be fairly concluded as having valid basis. Though it may be supposed that these states were for the most part entered into intentionally, the possibility must remain open to the fact of accidental inducement, perhaps by eating an unknown fungus or ingesting a concoction prepared by an ill-wisher.

Most individuals belonged to a group in some fashion or another. Whether they were freely born or adopted members of it, slaves or captives of war would have had an influence if they produced rock art.   Language, while not being a directly demonstrable influence on petroicons in general, may none the less have had an influence. Some groups would speak only one language, while others may have been multilingual. Individuals within a group may have spoken the same language as the group, a different language because of marriage or abduction or both.   Groups who spoke entirely different languages sometimes shared common territory as either friends or enemies. We may speculate that these differences had an influence on the making of petroicons and hence that the icons themselves may have had differing degrees of comprehension and meaning among the variations of lingual groups.

Mobility and function would have varied depending on the nature of the society itself. Certainly the family and extended family would have been the nucleus of any group and expansions of that somewhat dependent upon the nature of the group lifestyle. Broadly speaking, for purpose of discussion here, we may classify them in one of two ways— hunter/gathers or agrarian. The degree of mobility between the two is the factor that immediately sets them apart, with the first obviously covering considerable more territory than the later more sedentary mode. Consequently the function of petroicons may have been quite different in the two types of groups. In both cases though, rock art may have served as a tool to focus group unity and common values. It may have illustrated how a group was organized, instilled a sense of belonging to the group of those who understood the symbols, served as reassurance of group knowledge about periodic insecurities such as drought or eclipses or insured that necessary tasks were undertaken that would insure the survival of the group.

It is easy to envision for instance, an agrarian who may need to disperse food resources on an equitable basis among group members producing some system of tallying that distribution. If gardens were in close proximity to others it may have been necessary to distinguish one's own plot from another's with a map of sorts. If an irrigation ditch needed to be dug, perhaps a petroiconic map of its course was made. If certain resources required complex processing to become useful, such as the construction of mats or nets, it is not an unreasonable assumption that pictures of the process or the finished product may have been useful in the process of teaching others how to achieve the desired results. Marks would have been made to record astronomical events such as solstices and equinoxes that would have been important to know for the successful raising of crops. Magical rain making ceremonies and rituals may have been accompanied by the making of rock art.

Hunter gatherer groups, may have had even more reason for the production of petroicons. Maps and travel directions come immediately to mind as being important. Markers for resources like under ground springs that may not have been visible year around would have been important. As would have been markers of where caches of materials or tools were left for future use. It is safe to say that at least some, particularly food, resources may have been regarded as belonging to a particular group and this may have been indicated by a petroiconic marker. Through out the landscape there are numerous hidden dangers such as avalanches or flash floods whose known

37

existence may have provoked the making of warning signs.

All of these functions that rock art could have served, would have to have been consciously produced by an individual or more than one individual who understood the importance, meaning and purpose of the petroicons in regard to the particular group.

We have explored some of the ideas about who made rock art. Let us now turn our attention to the corollary idea of for whom were they made.

Once again we are presented with some basic choices. They could have been made for no one— idle doodles without meaning. They could have been produced for reasons that mattered only to the individual making them. Or produced for one other person or a small group of people with a limited relationship to the producer. Images may have been made for the group, or part of the group, to which the individual belonged or with whom they identified. Some perhaps were made to communicate with "spirit" beings with whom there could be   no "physical" relationship. Others might have been left to communicate with future generations or with individuals or groups who later followed through the same landscape. Or they may have been made to communicate with strangers who may have been friends or foes.   In each case, the audience of intended attention would have influenced what glyphs were made and their location. We can be nearly certain that we who look upon the rock art today were not the intended audience. But they have meanings for us none-the-less.   Whether that meaning is part of our archaeological studies, a part of national or regional heritage or simply an appreciation of their aesthetic beauty, we are their inheritors and it is up to us to preserve them with care and dignity.

40

CHAPTER TWO

WHERE WAS ROCK ART MADE?

Mankind has made marks on stones nearly every where it has been on the planet. One of the fundamental facets that must be examined to arrive at an understanding of the meanings and purposes of rock art is where it is located in the landscape.

The first and very obvious answer is on stone surfaces. What variables this includes will be discussed first. Two primary things stand out. The surface must have been suitable and it must have been accessible.

The suitability of a surface would have been dependent upon the method employed to make the glyph and the stone itself. The manufacture of pictographs would have been much easier on a smooth light colored surface, although any surface to which the pigment would adhere and bind could have been used. Many pictographs endure until the present because the surface on which they exist is relatively well protected from weathering. Petroglyphs would have been most easily produced on rocks with a desert varnish or patina on the surface, but could also have been made on virtually any stone as long as stone of equal or harder density was available to break the surface. Desert varnish is a very thin dark mineral rind that forms very slowly as a result of interaction with minerals, water and heat on the surface of many types of stone. When that surface layer is breached through pecking, scratching or abrading, the lighter stone beneath is exposed. In both cases, a clean surface, rather than one which may have been periodically exposed to such things as mud, would have been preferred. And in both cases, the more smooth the actual surface, the easier it would be to make marks.

Since glyphs may be of virtually any size, any surface even marginally bigger could have been employed. Of course, intended visibility would have played a role in this aspect.   In most cases the naturally occurring surface would have been used, although it is not unreasonable to suppose that some surfaces may have been prepared to some extent, i.e. surface accumulations of mud, lichen and debris may have been removed.

Features such as cracks in the rock, stains, vugs (small holes,) bumps, outcrops and edges would certainly have played a part in the placing of petroicons. Whether these were avoided or worked around, or actually incorporated into the image itself would have been a decision the individual producer would have needed to make.

Accessibility to the area where the images were made is an important consideration. Doubtlessly, there were images produced on smaller "portable" rocks and depending upon their size, may have been moved about in the landscape. However most rock art that we are aware of is located in a stationary setting. It is important to keep in mind that landscape elevations and other features may have changed considerably from the time the images were made and now. Surface levels may have been altered due to drifting soils, erosion by wind and water, changes in water courses and surface levels of water accumulations in lakes and marshes. Features such as lake shores and tidal plains may have varied considerably, even during very short periods of time, due to prevailing weather and moisture patterns. Consequently our description of locations may vary considerably from what the actual conditions were when the glyphs were produced and any determination based on function of location must be approached with caution. Some of the locations in which we find rock art today seem inaccessible but that may be because of the influences just mentioned.

We might further consider accessibility in terms of indoor and out door settings. Indoor in this case designating the interiors of spaces such as caves and rock shelters. Out door settings are obvious and require little further explanation. At just about any elevation, in just about any landscape and the transition areas between them, suitable rock surfaces have been used as the surface upon which to place petroicons. They may have been placed on a single surface or on a group of surfaces in close proximity to one another or on boulders large and small that were quite isolated. In some locations, glyphs may be found on both panels that are near one another and on outlier boulders some distance from the site. The interiors of caves both shallow and deep have been used as canvases in spite of the challenges of entering, creatures such as bears that may have inhabited them and the issue of how to create light in sufficient quantity to facilitate movement inside. Did the depth within the cave where the images were placed have a bearing on their meaning? Some caves have very unique acoustical properties. What part might echoes have played in the choices for rock art placement? On the interior walls of rock shelters, usually much less deep than caves, and around the entrances to them, petroicons were placed. Such shelters often have very extensive periods of occupation, both interrupted and continuous. Entrances may have undergone repeated blockages and clearings from blowing soils and/or rising and falling water levels and from large chunks of rock falling from the ceiling. Other earth movements, such as landslides, within the shelter itself may have changed the accessibility of some locations on its walls.

When we consider the where abouts of rock art, we must think about it in relationship to three different things. First, what is the location of the site itself? Second, what is the location of a given panel with in the site? And third, what is the location of each element on the panels? As well as there being a specific locus for each of the three, consideration must be given to their relationship with other sites, panels and glyphs in the landscape; and, in the case of panels and elements, to other panels and elements within the site.

As a complement to this information, place may be designated as public or private. Public locations may be in positions obvious to all, positions obvious to those who know where to look in a specific place for them or obvious to anyone passing through the nearby landscape. Private locations may be intentionally hidden or hidden by their remote location.

Further, some sites, panels or elements may be located to exploit a particular property of the locus itself. High points in the landscape and other positions lending themselves to the power of superior view are obvious. Both the ability to be seen and the ability to see from such places may have been relevant. Less frequent are sites that have unique acoustical properties, such as "bell" rocks which make a distinctive sound when struck and sites where extraordinary echo effects are facilitated. Some glyph sites are located near ocean shores so that they are intentionally periodically covered and uncovered by water. Others are situated so as to utilize openings through rocks and/or features on the horizon to mark astronomical events.

As just mentioned, for some sites the landscape itself dictates the location. The site may be in a place such as a cave that automatically delimits it. Such a site may be isolated from any other like it, or, if there are other similar caves around, it may be one of a series. Because caves can become hidden over time due to landslides or rising tidal levels, it may not always be easy to determine such relationships. The same may be said of rock shelter locations. Sites in convenient locations of passages through mountain passes, canyon walls or other elevationally different areas that have no alternative logical places of access, are in locations dictated by the landscape features.

Other sites may exist in a particular place because of their location near a survival resource such as food or water. Since, depending on the size and consistency of the resource availability, the site may have been used over long periods of time and by many people, often sites containing a substantial number of glyphs are present. Even such sources with less sustaining ability were often important and people using them made glyphs marking their usage.

A subsidiary idea here is that a glyph site may be present to mark the availability of a resource whose presence may not be immediately apparent.   A subsurface water source being an example.

Some sites exist, often many in close proximity to one another, because they are located where people spent considerable amounts of time together, either in sedentary village settings or in gathering at resource rich areas such as places where tubers or roots grew profusely. A series of sites with different resources were often visited during the course of the annual food gathering rounds. Other sites are located where very limited resources, particularly water, were available, often on an intermittent basis like after a rain storm. Such sites would have been of value to a very limited number of people at any given time, but as they were used repeatedly over time, accumulated glyphs made by the people who used them. Sites such as these are widely dispersed over landscapes and while public, are none the less quite isolated. Rock art may also have been made to indicate the location of caches of harvested recourses near the site of the harvest so they could be readily located upon return.

Some places in the landscape are particularly well adaptable by hunters seeking to harvest game animals. Natural passageways animals would use to access water and the water holes themselves would have been places hunters would have frequented and left their marks. What role those marks may have played in the actual hunt will be discussed else where.

Any where movement of people took place between various settings in the landscape, particularly over long distances, it is conceivable they may have left behind marks making it easier for those who followed, or themselves in the future, to retrace their steps. Hence places where decisions as to direction of travel would have been required would be obvious places where petroicons could have been placed to aid in such choices. Actual maps of passage ways through territories such as river drainages may have been made. What were the limits of a given individual or a group's geographic perception? Such limits as mountain ranges or impassable canyons or deserts may have been indicated by such map like drawings. At other locations where potential travel hazards such as flash floods or snake dens may have been present, the marks left were at geographically dictated locations.

Some marks left on stones may be only marks left behind by utilitarian functions—these would have been very much site defined. Certain pits and grooves maybe present because the powdered rock obtained had utilitarian value such as an abrasive or a medicine, or a particular magical quality pertaining to fecundity or rainfall. Certain serration patterns interpreted as petroicons may have been necessary to effectively process foods such as fish oil or fruit pulps on particular stones that would have been located in the proximity of the harvest. Some petroglyphs made on grinding slicks may have been made to increase the efficiency of the grinding process. If one were processing a food resource such as nuts that had a tough shell or husk it is easy to imagine how a depression that would hold the unprocessed food stationary would have been an aid in process of extracting the valued part.

Now let us turn our attention to the location of rock art panels within a site. As with rock art sites, panels may be public and obvious, private and hidden or private or public and remote. It is often difficult to explain why one rock surface contains a panel while a nearby surface of seeming equal quality contains none. Discovery of some relationships between panels may be dependent on the time of day or the time of year when they are viewed due to changing light conditions. Was this coincidental or intentional on the part of the makers?

Obviously the first consideration is where within the site rock art surfaces that are suitable for the placement of rock art are located. At some sites such locations are very limited either by the amount or nature of the stone itself. At others there is a vast and sometimes seemingly endless array of possible surfaces available. Frequently at such sites not only is there a linear element involved, such as a miles-long basaltic rim, but also varying degrees of elevation in relation to the current surface level. Again we need to remind ourselves that current surface level may be considerably different from what it was when the glyphs were made. At some sites, panels, or portions of panels lay well hidden below the current surface and are only revealed when the site is excavated.   As regards meaning, the question must be posed, was there a hierarchy of significance in where the panel was located. That is, were panels at higher elevations within a site more significant than those on lower levels? Was there a "beginning" or "entrance way" to a site and if so were panels located in closer proximity to that of greater importance? Was the fact that some panels within a site can be reached only with considerable skill, dexterity and ingenuity (such as climbing) indicative of increased significance? Were glyphs on a panel that were in spaces such as thin cracks between boulders or very small caves and were only accessible to individuals of a certain stature of increased importance? Some panels are located in places where only one individual at a time may view them. How did the glyphs in such spaces differ from those in spaces where many could view the glyphs at the same time? Was the angle at which the observer would need to look, up for instance, in order to see the panel taken into consideration by the maker?

Rock art is found on panels facing all directions, not only of the compass but also up and down and at varying inclinations dictated by the surface. Of what importance, if any, was the direction in which the panel faced? This direction would have dictated, in many cases, the angle and area from which the glyphs on it could be viewed. At a particular site, was there a sequence in which the panels were intended to be viewed? Certainly if one accepts the idea that some panels are meant to record certain astronomical events, such as solstices, the direction the panel faces would be of tantamount importance. Of particular importance at such sites would have been the syntax so to speak of the glyphs themselves. Were they meant to be "read" from right to left or vise versa or from up to down or the reverse.

What part did the play of light caused by holes, cracks, outcrops and edges play in the placement of panels? Light daggers caused by sunlight passing through narrow spaces and casting rays on a surface may have prompted the making of glyphs by their seeming movement. Shadows may have found significance in a similar manner. Glyphs on such panels may have been made so that they were either illuminated at certain times by the light and conversely hidden at others by shadows. What part did artificial light from campfires or torches and lamps have in the placement of panels? Were the illusion of 3-D or "moving" glyphs using light and shadow ever intended as part of a panel's purpose?

Were there techniques employed in the manufacture of certain petroicons that were deliberately intended to trick or mislead the eye into believing it was seeing something different from different angles. Double images, or a image in negative and positive relief may have been used for such effects. The effects of figure ground relationships probably played a part as well. The actual shape of the stone itself may have been modified in some cases to aid in the production of such effects. In some cases elements from one glyph are incorporated into another so that depending upon one's particular point of view, one sees one of the two glyphs or alternatively, one and then the other.

If a particular rock formation strongly resembles a face or an animal, were panels placed on such stones to reinforce the resemblance or was such practice avoided out of deference to the likeness? Could this preference have differed depending on the particular belief system of the maker? Were other manifestations of pareidolia (vague and random stimulus eliciting a psychological phenomena that perceives the stimulus as significant) such as stains on rocks, differences in rock color or lichen patterns involved in the process of choosing the location of panels?

Were some panels deliberately placed in out-laying locations associated with other panels at a site? Was this done to conceal the panel or render it difficult to see by the casual observer? Were some panels deliberately placed in places where only the informed would know where to look for them because they indicated the location of hidden caches of tools or food?

As a final aspect about the where of rock art, we need to examine individual elements. Where they were placed at the site, on the panel and in relation to other glyphs may all have been considerations affecting their meaning.

Were elements at one site placed so as to point in the direction that would lead to other sites? Would the element itself be a repetition of a glyph that occurred at another site indicating a relationship or continuity between them?

Might elements be made so that they faced other elements on other panels at the same site, indicating a combined meaning? Or meaning from occupying the space between them? Might elements be made in such a manner that they related to other elements on the same panel? Two anthropomorphs facing one another, or an anthropomorph facing away from a zoomorph might be examples of such a relationship.

Some elements, such as a series of dots or short lines are quite obviously meant to have a relationship with one another. If elements are connected to one another by lines can we assume a relationship. Further, might that relationship be defined by the shape or thickness of the line it self? Did a thicker connecting line indicate a stronger connection than a thinner one?

If a particular element was repeated many times at a site, what did that indicate? Was that petroicon made by the same person or by different people? At the same time or at subsequent times? Did repetition of a glyph strengthen or duplicate its power as it was repeatedly made at the same time or over a period of time?

Are elements touching each other and if so where? Was this intentional or accidental? Were they so arranged by the original producer or was the touching produced by a later production of a glyph on the same panel? And was that done intentionally or incidentally? What was the relationship when elements were superimposed over other elements? In some cases might this have indicated an intention on the part of the second maker to negate the meaning of the earlier glyph? Might meaning have been intended by the sandwiching of a glyph between two others? For example, perhaps a closed grid like a tick-tac-toe game box was drawn first, then an animal over the top of it, and then another grid on top—

54

could that have been a way of expressing that an animal was caught between two nets? It has been suggested that perhaps some touching was in imitation of certain universally understood sign language signals.

On some panels, the "correct" or "right side up" orientation of the individual elements is obvious because there is only a certain angle from which the panel may be observed. On panels such as these, what significance may be attached to elements whose orientation is different, either side ways or even "upside down" in relation to the whole panel? What determined the "correct" orientation of elements on panels such as on low boulders where there is no single point of view? Was position of an element in relation to the edges of the surface, to holes in it or to cracks something that influenced meaning? In reference to the later, we know that many peoples believed that the underworld could be reached by entering such surface features and that animals such as lizards, because of their ability to traverse such features, were thought to have associated powers. If elements had a relationship to other elements on the same panel did that extend to all of them on the panel or only a specific distance? If meaning was influenced by any of these things, was that meaning generally perceived or was it intelligible only to those trained to be able to understand the meaning?

55

Was the element made deliberately so that it had a relationship with light and/or shadows as discussed above concerning panels? It seems quite evident that in some sites with light daggers or shadows present that spirals were designed to either highlight or record their apparent movement.

Where elements were placed in relation to "architectural" elements at site, such as above entrances to caves or passageways may have had influence on meaning, such as welcoming those who entered or warning others not to enter.

The placement of elements as well as their size would determine from what distance the petroicon could have been seen. That too may have been part of the message the maker intended to express.

It may have been that glyphs on a panel had no relationship to one another, they were simply there because of the availability of the canvas. This was probably magnified at panels that were used over long periods of time, particularly if that usage was by different groups of people. The attitude toward previous users would certainly have been a factor effecting placement.

The type of landscape, desert, mountain, steppe or lowlands, and all the various types between, would have a great deal of influence on nearly every facet of the lives of people inhabiting them. Those geographical differences had an influence on where rock art was placed. Consider for instance how many rocks suitable for the placement of rock art might exist in a swampy low land as compared to a high mountainous area. Not all rock surfaces are suitable for the making of rock art. Did the type of rocks or individual rocks themselves that were suitable have meaning as well as purpose?

CHAPTER THREE

WHEN WAS ROCK ART MADE?

The temporal context in which rock art was made is the next facet we shall explore in our attempt to discover the factors that influence meaning. We have two points of view from which we may approach the question of when. The first is from the view point of the rock art researcher. The second is from the point of view of the maker of the petroicons—what was the temporal influence that caused the images to be made? That may have been quite personal, relating perhaps to the person's age or an occurrence of importance in their life, or it may have been made in response to temporal events such as sunsets or rises.

Two types of dating are possible from the researchers' perspective—absolute and relative. Both are important because they help determine by whom, or at least, by what group or archaeologically defined type of people produced them. That information aids in understanding meaning because of the variations of actual activities and pursuits of different types of groups.

Absolute is the more difficult of the two. Because pictographs may contain organic matter that can be radio carbon dated, it is less problematic than petroglyphs, which don't.   Since binders such as blood, urine and pitch may have been used in the preparation of pigments for pictographs, small samples may yield results that give a date with a narrow field of error. As this technique continues to be refined it yields increasingly more significant results. Dating of petroglyphs relies on less precise methods. At times, if petroicons occur in the same stratigraphic layer as other cultural remains such as campfire lenses, shell middens or artifacts, they can be assumed to be at least as old as that layer. Some geological markers such as ash from volcanic eruptions provide a convenient reference point from which the date of petroicons can be more or less determined. Many new techniques involving such things as desert rind (patina or desert varnish) analysis and lichen growth research are showing promise as ways in which we may in the future better determine the age of petroglyphs.

Relative dating can be done in a number of ways, although each of them only gives us an age reference in terms of a particular glyph's relationship to other glyphs. If one glyph is superimposed on another, it may be logically concluded that the newer one is on top. In general, although variations due to weathering or water exposure are present, glyphs that are more heavily repatinated (have a darker layer of desert varnish reformed on them) are older than those on the same panel that are less so. Some events such as the replacement of the atlatl by the bow and arrow and the arrival of horses in North America are associated with dates that are quite reliable. When glyphs are found depicting them, reliable relative dating is possible.

When we examine the temporal context from the point of view of the maker of rock art, analysis becomes more complex. To make this task more manageable, we may begin by breaking it down into the standard categories of past, present and future. Some might argue that prehistoric man had conceptions of time that did not follow this structure; be that as it may, for our purpose here, we shall assume that, whatever their description, it still encompassed that familiar "line." Within each of these three we may further delineate to what extent the intent was to be temporary or permanent. At any given site there are three possible temporal relationships of glyphs there—none (they were all made independently and for unrelated reasons and only for the maker and perhaps others in the immediate present,) continual (meaning was intended to be conveyed to all who saw them in what ever time frame they saw them,) and progressive (they were intended to convey meaning to those who observed them at some time in the future.)

These categories may be further refined by associating elements, panels and sites with property, records, activities or occasions. Observers of the markings might have distinguished between the various temporal intentions of the maker by having learned traditions associated with the site, its location when they encountered it or by hearing oral expression of intention directly from the maker. Perhaps the easiest way to explore these ideas is to give a hypothetical example of each.

Past, permanent: marks intended to indicate the death of a person are intended to be permanent markers about an event that is in the past.

Past, temporary: water was located here two feet underground when we passed this way, by leaving these marks it is hoped that we will remember and you will know where it is.

Present, permanent: these marks indicate that this is where all human waste is to be disposed.

Present, temporary: these marks indicate this is how many fish we caught today and how many each of you may take with you.

Future, permanent: all who see these marks should know that this marks a boundary of territory that our group claims.

Future, temporary: when the second group in our hunting party follows us tomorrow these marks will tell them we went this direction and that they should go the other.

Now let us look at some examples of time in relation to records, property, activities and occasions. Since this is a somewhat arbitrary division, there may be overlaps in some of the ideas. People following the original makers at a later time would be able to interpret the marks through several methods. If the time gap were small between maker and observer, the meaning may have been conveyed through personal oral communication. If it were longer, group oral traditions may have served the purpose. Or in either case, certain marks may have had some degree of "universal" understanding over wide areas and wide periods of time by virtue of the fact they expressed universal ideas. For instance, no matter what further modifiers may be attached, pointing a finger up means up and pointing a finger down means down. Pointing a finger at one's self indicates a reference to self.

Records: let us suppose that, due to drought conditions for instance, a group was forced to migrate. What ever rock art that group had produced while living there would be a record of the past when either they or their descendants returned or new people inhabited the land. Let us suppose you were the vanguard of a migrating group, and after much reconnoitering you had discovered a place that was acceptable to locate. You might leave marks there so that when the rest of the group arrived, if you were not there, they would know that the particular spot had been chosen. A similar group might make marks to indicate to those who followed that large herds of game had been sighted nearby a specific location. When a group arrived at a new location, one of the group might make a record of how many people had arrived with them or how many horses they had brought for instance. A single unique event such as a supernova or a very bright comet passing might be occasion to make a mark to record the event. Or an individual may have seen the biggest rattlesnake he had ever seen and drawn a picture of it to record the occasion; a particularly large game animal may have been harvested and a similar record made. Perhaps a series of events such as a flash flood occurred and killed several members of the group and someone in the group made a rock art record of this event. Perhaps a number of food caches were made a moderate distance from a habitation site and someone made a record of how many of these sites there were and their locations as a mnemonic device for themselves and/or others. The locations of the sites themselves may have been recorded by glyphs a certain distance from the sites themselves. Similar glyphs may have been made to mislead or misguide others about the locations of caches.   The same glyphs may be made repeatedly for a number of reasons—to simply record that something had occurred more than once, as inducement to make something happen again, or as inducement to make something stop occurring.

Property: while ownership as we know it today was probably a concept which had not developed , it is likely that even small groups regarded some portion of the landscape as being more closely associated with their group rather than with others. This may have been through decades or even hundreds of years of a group utilizing the resources of a particular area or through banishment of peoples who occupied the area when the invading group arrived or through acquisition by intermarriage. In all of these cases marks may have been made on stone to signify proprietary rights. It is not inconceivable that as a defense mechanism against hostile groups that certain strategically important places such as passes and river fords may have been marked so that their perceived control would be known. Certain fishing grounds or root or seed gathering locations may not only have "belonged" to certain groups, but also to families or individuals within a group and that designation may have been marked on the stones. Rock art may have been produced to record return visits by either a group or an individual to a particular place in a landscape. To show generational links to a particular landscape there might have been father/son or mother/daughter glyphs that served to show those relationships.

Occasion: even today humans tend to note different occasions in special ways.   Perhaps the manufacture of petroicons was at least part of the process of marking occasions in the past as well. Celebratory occasions quickly come to mind— birthdays, marriages, anniversaries and graduations are generally acknowledged as occasions worth noting and have attendant rituals associated with them. As has been previously noted, ritual played an important part in some magical practices and therefore shamans or medicine people may have left images behind on stone that were meant to either evoke or celebrate the arrival of particular outcomes such as rain or a bountiful supply of game animals. Ordinary individuals may well have marked special occasions such as births, multiple births or coming of age acknowledgments with the production of glyphs. There is no reason not to believe that, at least in some societies, the union of two individuals in what today we would consider matrimony, may not have been celebrated by making pictographs or petroglyphs. Perhaps some petroicons were made by women to keep track of ovulation cycles so that forms of rhythmical birth control could be facilitated. Other occasions such as deaths and funerary proceedings were also taken note of by the manufacture of images on stone. And some petroicons may have been made so that the deceased would be remembered, much as grave markers are widely used today.

Noteworthy biographical occasions to both groups and individuals may have been recorded by the making of rock art. Visitation by personages held in high esteem by a group may have been noted, as might have visits by malevolent forces such as raiding enemies or people bringing sickness or bad luck. The fortune or misfortunes of battles or organized hunts, as well as the mechanics and number of people involved, may have been recorded in celebration or lament, by individuals or groups, as an immediate expression of the occasion or as a means by which knowledge of the event could be preserved for the future. Large gathering, particularly of people from different groups, may have been noted, as would have been such things as territorial agreements or treaties. Some rock art, perhaps later perceived as decorative, may have been made as a simple social activity to employ hands while visiting.

Let us for a moment imagine that an individual or a small group was separated by either plan or accident from the larger group with which it was associated. And further that it was expected that at some point in the future the larger group would follow. What type of occasional markers may have been left behind on the stones at any given location?   Signals that conveyed, "arrived here or arrived here from," "stayed or waited here," "left here," "headed there," "will return here or not return here," and some kind of time indicator for these actions would logically have been left on the stones.

Activity: there is a wide range of activities, both social and solitary, during which petroicons might have been produced.   For both groups and individuals, one of three states of consciousness would have been evident during activities: a normal day to day living state, a stressed state or an induced state. The first is pretty much self explanatory and would have been present during food acquisition, preparation and consumption, rest and movement. A stressed state may have been caused by many factors including being pursued by enemies or animals, starvation or water deprivation. An induced state would be deliberate in nature, being produced by such things as voluntary fasting, self-inflicted pain, drumming or ingestion of psychoactive plant substances.

During "normal" times when many people gathered to harvest food resources such as bulbs or berries there was usually considerable social interaction on the part of hunter/gatherer societies. During such times many ideas, as well as goods from diverse locations, were probably exchanged. If the group were large, then making a symbol on stone near your camping location showing what it was you had for exchange may have been employed—the sandal maker, perhaps, showing a symbol for sandals. Games may have been played during such times and perhaps scores were recorded. Tally marks may have been necessary when large numbers of goods were being exchanged or resources gathered in one place that would have been dispersed when the harvest was complete. Some of these activities might have gone on at less sedentary gathering places such as villages as well. There, marks may have been made on stone incidental to some necessary activity like removing the oil from fish; they may have been made for decorative purposes; as relief from boredom (graffiti) ; or for amusement purposes (maybe to entertain young ones by making it easier for them to visualize animals. Adolescent boys in particular may have made erotic images for masturbatory purposes.) Rock art imagery may also reflect virility and fertility. Either celebration of these or as signs to enhance or cause them. Some glyphs may have served as examples (net and basketry patterns, for instance) for others learning a skill or process. Individuals, particularly children, may have made images just for the self rewarding experience of having been able to do so.

During "stressed" times petroicons may have been produced as pleas to higher powers to have the stress of starvation or thirst alleviated by the use of sympathetic magic. Talismanic magic may have been used an aid in protection from animals or enemies. Or petroicons may have been manufactured to simply record the time of stress or its duration or results. In some cases, the means by which the stress was alleviated may have been the subject for glyphs.

During "induced" times many factors such as fasting, extreme pain or exhaustion (sometimes self induced) may have caused the individual to experience visions. During such periods (sometimes referred to as vision quests) imagery that was experienced through hallucination or dreaming may have been replicated by petroicons. Images may have been made to actually facilitate the visions or to record the fact they had taken place. It is very likely that shamans or other knowledgeable people used psychoactive plants during quests or rituals as aids in the experience of visions. Repetitive activities such as drumming and dancing might also have produced induced states of consciousness These too would have been noted in a similar manner. There is a school of thought that hypothesizes that there are certain universally present phosphines that humans experience during trauma to the eyes or during drug induced reveries and these are the origin of many universally present glyphs such as spirals and circles. Much more actual research needs to be done before this idea can become fully tenable, but it is a possibility. Such induced altered states may well have been the results of accidental head trauma or fervors caused by illness and in each case may have caused the individual to see patterns of an abstract nature that they tried to duplicate with petroicons. If any of this imagery was thought to have power, either malevolent or benevolent, it may have been reproduced else where after the original experience in hopes of evoking the power again.

In this portion of our discussion we have seen that markings on rock have been intentionally produced during a broad spectrum of temporal periods in response to a large number of stimuli—in fact, they were made at all and any times—and that to understand their meaning and purpose, that "when" is an important consideration. It is an important facet both from the maker's point of view and from our own as we seek to further our comprehension.

Above: Dave Campa photograph

CHAPTER FOUR

HOW WAS ROCK ART MADE?

In exploring how rock art was made and how that relates to its meaning, we can examine the question from three perspectives: first, the basic, physical, material process including the substances and tools used and what influence they may have had, both during the process and afterwards; secondly, what may have influenced and inspired the glyph producers to make the images they did; and finally, how did the elements relate to others, both on the same panel, at nearby panels or to panels at other sites.

Rock art is generally thought of as being either pictographs or petroglyphs. Frequently a third type, geoglyphs, is added to the list. Marks made by inscribing wet mud or clay are sometimes included in the definition as well.

Let us look at the last two first. Mud glyphs, as they are referred to, are often not much more than traces left by fingers and hands being dragged through wet clay or mud. In places protected from weathering, such as cave interiors, such marks may last for a long time. They are frequently made by children as evidenced by the size of the fingers making them and we may suppose that, just as now, some children are fascinated by making "finger paintings" that may have been the case in ages past. More representational images have been found and these were frequently executed by holding two or more fingers together while making the image, leaving more or less parallel lines (digital tracings) to delineate the figure. Some glyphs of this type appear to have been made by the dragging of a sharp object through the medium. At times evidently a combination of the two techniques was used. Frequently, images that are clearly representational, such as rattlesnakes, are found amongst what appear to be abstract meanders. Markings similar to those found on pottery may have had similar significance when properly analyzed. More complex figures such as anthropomorphs have been discovered that may in fact "tell a story" by their decorations or accouterments. They are found both in residual mud banks and in thin layers of mud that sometime cover the walls and ceilings of caves. The practice seems not one that is widespread, probably due to the limited number of caves containing such materials. If there were a "tradition" surrounding the manufacture of such images, it is not unimaginable that there may have been a hierarchy of importance of sorts attached to how many fingers were actually used in making them. Collaborative efforts at such sites also seem easy to imagine.

In many places, particularly South American coastal desert regions, the rocks and earth on the surface take on a dark "patina" or "desert varnish" due to constant exposure to the sun. In some places people have methodically moved surface rocks aside exposing the lighter earth beneath. This results in a form of image making called geoglyphs, that is sometimes included as being a type of rock art. In places, these representational figures, often zoomorphs or anthropomorphs, are very large and some abstract lines may even stretch across landscapes for many miles. They are particularly intriguing in that some are placed in such terrain that the images can not be seen unless one is in the air above them. (There are no higher geological elevations nearby from which they are visible.) There are a good many theories as to their purpose, ranging from very far fetched, space aliens made them, to perhaps more reasonable purposes such as cleared ways for ceremonial dances or other rites. Others believe they may have been connected in some way with elaborate irrigation systems. Since a considerable amount of physical energy would have been necessary to move large amounts of stone even short distances, it seems likely that the process was a group undertaking rather than an individual one. Although we can only guess at what meanings these glyphs may have had, perhaps the animals were clan totems for instance, since a major expenditure of energy was involved in their construction, they most assuredly had meaning for those who caused them to be made. Whether those who did the actual labor understood the full meaning or not remains a mystery.

The majority of the rock art in the world is either petroglyphs or pictographs. In short, petroglyphs are made by disturbing the surface of rock and pictographs are made by applying pigment to the surface. While there are a good many things the two methods have in common, each has its own unique characteristics that must be considered when thinking about meaning. We shall discuss them separately here.

Petroglyphs are made by physically disturbing the surface of the stone to some degree of depth. Many types of stone upon which petroicons are found have a surface that is darker than the underlying stone itself. This patination is due to various combinations of heat, light, moisture and mineral dust in the places they are located. In most cases the production by nature of this "patina" or "desert varnish" is a very, very slow process, often taking thousands of years. Even when this patina is of great age, it is rarely more than several microns thick.   In most cases petroglyphs are formed by piercing that patina to reveal the lighter stone beneath, although there are traditions that instead remove stone from the space around the darker patina to leave the image visible as darker than the surrounding space. In both cases, the disruption of the surface may be caused by scratching, incising, abrading, drilling or pecking of the surface. In some circumstances a combination of methods may be used. While it is possible to produce results with a stone of the same kind, the task is made much more efficient if the tool is of harder stone than the medium upon which it is being used. That fact, in a primitive mind, may have given the tool stone "power" that the receiving stone was complimentary with or in subordination to. Quartz for instance is a relatively hard stone that is found in a large variety of places and when it is stuck it luminesces or lights up. It is unlikely that properties such as this and sparks created by the violent interaction of some stones would have gone unnoticed. Tool stones may have been of a number of different types. A simple point on a harder stone would make it able to scratch or incise another stone and of course repetition would have increased the effect. It may well be that some marks on stones may be nothing more than "tool sharpening" marks and really have nothing at all to do with the primary subject here. Much blunter stones could have been used to abrade lines as well, even stone of the same kind could have achieved this. Drilling of small holes by rotation of a sharp harder

77

stone was another method by which either a single hole or a series may have been produced. Some of these holes may have subsequently been connected by removal of rock left between them. "Bits" of stone used as such tools may have been affixed to wooden shafts to make rotation either by hands alone or using a bow more efficient. In some cases, it may not have been the hole itself or the pattern of holes that was important but rather the powder or dust that was removed; it may have been used for its medicinal or pigmentation qualities. Pecking may have been accomplished by simply holding a rock in one's hand and repeatedly striking the surface in the same or consecutive places until the desired effect had been achieved. Or one rock may have been held much like a chisel against the reciprocating surface and struck repeatedly with a "hammer stone." Each of these methods doubtlessly was somewhat dependent upon the preference of the maker and perhaps even more so upon what materials were available. In all cases, it is not unreasonable to believe that a significance beyond the end result may have been assigned to the process itself with perhaps appropriateness to the occasion being a consideration. In some societies, the simple fact of breaking the surface may have been equated with breaching the membrane that separates the upper and lower worlds. By taking this action, and/or touching the results, it might have been believed that access could be gained to that other world. Some scratches and other abrasions were doubtlessly produced incidentally as people experimented with different types of stone tools and methods of making more purposeful images.

Pictographs are made by applying pigments to a stone surface. Many different materials were used in the manufacture of these pigments and each may have had meaningful connotations that, at least in part, dictated their use. Almost universally available and utilized was ocher, an earthen iron oxide substance akin to rust, that has a special property that actually allows it to bond with other stones. Though predominately a spectrum of red shades, yellows and orange hues are also present and used. It is easy to see how particularly the bright red might have been associated with blood and have been assigned various meanings just like the real thing. One only has to think of bleeding wounds and funerary practices or menstrual blood and female coming of age rites to see how such connections may have been made. Black pigments would have been produced from charcoal or dark colored lichen or moss and in each of these cases meaning may have been assigned based on their origin. Other colors such as greens were obtained from colored clays and plant tissue and associations based on place of origin or properties of plants may have been assigned. These substances, after having been reduced to fine powder, were combined with a binding agent that may have been made from a variety of things including blood, urine or other bodily fluids and/or vegetable matter such as pitch or sap. It is easy to see how a belief that some part of the essence of the pigment creator would have been incorporated into the pigment and subsequent glyph if body fluids were used. In each case, these substances may have added a layer of meaning to the pigments used in the execution of pictographs. Each may have had appropriate and taboo occasions of employment. For instance, let us suppose that menstrual blood was incorporated into the manufacturing process for pigments used during puberty rites for females and that this was the tradition and would have been appropriate. Now let us imagine that a warrior might make marks on rocks before a battle that incorporated their own blood. Though both these examples employ blood, it is easy to see how taboo and appropriate apply.

These pigments were applied in a number of ways to stone surfaces and it is not unreasonable to suggest that the method of application would have been another part of the process to which meaning may have been given.

We may call one method of application stenciling. A hand or other body part or an object was placed flat on the surface and then the pigment was broadcast around it and on top of it by sprinkling, or blowing it from the mouth or through a tube so that when the hand or object was removed, its outline would be visible. Was this outline the object of the exercise, or was, perhaps the period of time during which the rock and the hand were one because they were the same color due to the pigment important? We know that in many societies there were beliefs about the realm of the underworld being inside rocks.

Fingers themselves were frequently used to apply the pigment and as a consequence many lines in rock art found throughout the world are the width of fingers. Brushes of various materials such as animal hair and plant fibers were also utilized. The purpose for which the petroicon was being produced may have dictated which method of application was appropriate. Some marks of pigment may also simply be incidental to the main process itself, like wiping excess pigment from an applicator, testing the color of the pigment or cleaning the fingers after the glyph had been made.

At some sites both petroglyphs and pictographs are present. Frequently they are not obviously directly associated with one another, although there are many places where the two techniques are combined. Petroglyphs may be "filled in" with pigment to make them more visible at the time they are made or added later to refresh or renew the image. No matter when the application took place, it would have been opportunity to add an additional layer of meaning to the glyphs.

Different meanings may have been assigned to the actual rock surface upon which the petroicons were being placed.   Most surfaces would have been natural, but in some cases would have been prepared to varying degrees, such as cleaning or smoothing. Would the meaning have dictated when such preparation was appropriate or even essential above and beyond the simple physical ability of the surface to receive the glyph?

Different methods of manufacturing petroicons would have taken different amounts of time to execute and different amounts of time to gather and prepare the tools and substances required to make them. Quality, as well as being a function of ability of the producer, would have been dependent upon the amount of time and care it took to make them. It is reasonable to assume that the time and the expenditure of energy would have had some meaning. This is may be illustrated by comparing the differential between a casual dot and the drawing of a circle. A few pecks in the same place in most cases, or a single touch of a finger would produce a dot simply and quickly. A circle on the other hand, would require some fore thought, such as making sure there was sufficient space available on the surface and perhaps an outline being drawn through recording the path of the rotation of a stick. While both the dot and circle are ideally scaled replicas of one another, their meaning and purpose due to the amount of energy required to make them must have also varied. By pure conjecture, we might imagine a dot meaning one and a circle meaning many; or that a circle indicated the same thing as a dot but of more or less importance.

We have seen then that there are many factors relating to the petroicons and the methods used in their manufacture that would have been opportunities for assigning meaning to either the tools, the medium or the process used in creation as well as the glyphs themselves. Today, an artist may have a favorite pen or brush that they use to most effectively produce certain results, may prefer pigment made of one material over that of others because of its light reflecting properties and may prefer to create on paper rather than canvas. For the artist, all of these choices have some relationship to the meaning and purpose of their work. So it has probably always been.

Let us turn our attention now to factors inherent in the nature of the environment that may have been involved in the inspiration for the making of petroicons. These too may have contributed to meaning.

83

Some of these factors would have been constant, others variable depending upon season and even time of day.   We should note that some of these "inspirations" are predicated on a propensity for humans to engage in a visual psychological phenomena   called pareidolia.   This involves an image or a sound being perceived as significant even though it is a random, often vague stimulus. Common occurrences of this are demonstrated by the seeing of animal or face shapes in clouds or by seeing the rabbit or man in the moon. Such perceptions may have been accidental or have been intentionally practiced; in either case meaning may have become associated.

Constantly present would have been things such as the shape of the stones themselves, the shapes of edges or combinations of edges and the shapes of cracks and their extensions. The perception of these would often have been dependent upon the angle at which they were viewed and hence the necessity of anyone who was to form a similar impression, sharing that point of view. Reflections in water, either permanent or temporary may have contributed to such perceptions. In some locations rock surfaces are prone to being covered to one extent or another with mineral stains that may leach from surrounding earth   and   rocks;   these   stains,   often   made progressively over time, are usually quite irregular in shape and may have suggested images. Animal urine also sometimes forms such stains. Lichen growth often has similar properties. Vugs—small holes or depressions in rock surfaces—either alone, or in combination with others, or other features, may have suggested certain patterns or images, or suggested the idea that such a feature could be enlarged. Scratches from such things as tree branches repeatedly moving in the wind or animals using a surface for a "scratching post" for either claws or antlers or horns may have suggested certain shapes that, when accentuated and embellished, became petroicons. On occasion, complex figure/ground relationships may have been noted and accentuated in the glyphs so that more than one interpretation was facilitated.   The classic modern example of the silhouettes of faces or vases might have had its counterpart during the Neolithic Age.

Less permanent, more dynamic factors that may have suggested shapes for the production of imagery are connected to light and shadow. Shadows from overhangs and edges change shape on the surface on which they appear, as well as appear to progress across the surface. This is often dependent not only on the time of day, but on the season during which the phenomena is observed. This may have narrowed the window of time in which the meaning intended by the maker could have been ascertained. This may have lead to the conception of using rock art for calenderical observations and computations. Complimentary to the idea of shadows, is the occurrence of light beams shaped by the terrain they either passed around or through. It has been demonstrated that some such occurrences were integral components at sites that sought to record astronomical events such as solstices and equinoxes. While these light/shadow events would have occurred outdoors, similar phenomena would have been observable in cave settings due to the use of torches or lamps. No matter the source, the results would have been a perception of movement and this in itself may have prompted the making of some imagery, perhaps to be highlighted by or to highlight it. The recurrence and the variability may both have taken on meaning. At the very least, the apparent movement would differentiate them from more static images and, although produced naturally, if explained by a story teller might take on supernatural meaning.

Images may have been inspired by other shapes that occur in nature such as cloud shapes, the shape of lightning strikes, the shape of the horizon or the shape of single or groups of trees or other plants. Other celestial events such as supernovas, comets, meteor showers, the phases of the moon, Borealis, eclipses of both the sun and moon and constellations may have provided inspiration. There are some who believe that in the far distant past certain large scale electrical plasmic events took place in the earth's atmosphere and may have been recorded.

Shapes may have been artificially created by the projection of shadows from body parts or other objects onto stone surfaces. In some cases a rough surface may have been thoroughly covered in pigment and then selectively brushed off, leaving lines and blobs that may have suggested either realistic or abstract shapes.

In some places on earth, fossils of both plants and animals are present at surface level. Upon seeing one of them, since it was already a marking on stone, might not one attempt to reproduce it and give that reproduction perhaps the same meaning as assigned to the original?

Not all imagery that is found depicted on rock art originated in that medium. Butchering of meat would have left knife cuts on bone which might have occasionally suggested other images. People from a wide variety of time and cultures have decorated their bodies with pigment, tattooing and scarification. It is not unlikely that some of these motifs and their accompanying meanings may have been transferred to stone. Crafts such as weaving, braiding and basket and net making have integral patterns that may have been transferred. Pottery was frequently decorated with designs, as were other tools and implements made of more perishable materials like wood, bark, fabric or bone. These designs too, may have been migrated to markings on stone.

While the focus on rock art is usually on the visual element, there is an aural component as well, particularly in regard to the making of petroglyphs. Some stones themselves make "ringing" tones when struck with other stones, which may have given rise to marks left behind from such activity. Some forms of rock art, perhaps long dot series or wave patterns, may have been meant to depict rhythms rather than forms. Sounds made by repetitive pecking on one stone by another would have certainly been suggestive of certain sounds produced by rattles, drums or bull-roarers. Perhaps certain patterns of pecking may have evoked a rhythm much as musical notation does today. In some cases this production of sound by officiants and/or participants, may have played a part in ceremonies or rituals performed by shamans, warriors or hunters. There is some evidence to suggest that certain animals are curious about unfamiliar sounds and may thus have been attracted by pecking sounds. If this were the case, then it would necessitate a different way of thinking about meaning and its relationship to rock art. It is not inconceivable that pictographs, although not actually producing sound, may have sought to depict it. There are certain landscapes that produce significantly louder echoes than normal and certain petroicons may exist as a result of that fact as well.

How the elements themselves are arranged on a given panel is our next point of consideration.

Several preliminary questions come to mind when examining this facet, each of which may have been opportunity for meaning to be attached to the petroicons themselves.

Were the elements produced all at the same time in a single, or closely sequential, session? Or were they made in some sort of cyclic sequence, or perhaps several cyclic sequences? Were the glyphs originals from the mind of the maker, copies of previous efforts by the same maker, or by a different maker. If they were copies, were they copied from the same panel, other panels at the same site, or copies from panels at a different site? Were they copied images with modifications? Were those modifications copies as well, or originals? Each of these instances would be a juncture where meaning may have varied between that originally intended and the subsequent versions.

Were originals and copies reflections of what was already fully formed in the mind of the makers before they began, or did some images take on other aspects as they were drawn? To envision how the later process may have taken place let us entertain a simple example. A maker of petroicons draws a circle, or comes across a circle already drawn. This suggests to him the shape of a face, so he adds two dots for eyes, this further suggests that a mouth shaped line should be added. He, or another glyph maker, comes to the panel at a later time and sees the dots as the pupils of eyes and adds a circle around them. Extrapolating from this, eventually we make have a stick figure, perhaps with details such as fingers and toes. Each part of this process, whether it was done by one or several people, had meaning attached to it. This may be further illustrated by an even simpler example: a single straight vertical line. Imagine the any number of ways in which that may be modified by one or more horizontal lines. The second line could cross at any point over the first, or perhaps only be adjacent to one side or the other. The angle at which it crossed could theoretically have three hundred and fifty-eight variations. Numerous lines increase the number of variables, each of which could have had specific meanings. Begin modifying those properties by such things as the thickness, or varying thickness of the individual lines, and the possible meanings become exponentially compounded. When interpreting what we perceive as a single image then, may in fact be a combination of many related images. And if there was in fact the case, the panel may have a more dynamic meaning much as the difference today between a still picture and a movie.

More will be discussed in the next chapter about what the glyphs actually depict, but for now let us simply keep in mind that they may be broadly classified as naturalistic, stylized or abstract. These types may exist by themselves on any given panel, or in combination with each other. And they may be originals or modified.

We can breakdown our discussion about how elements relate to one another by considering the following seven things: orientation, size, perspective, detail, connectivity, repetition and symmetry.

We can think of orientation in two ways. First, orientation on the panel itself and secondly, orientation to other glyphs on the same panel. Most panels will have a "logical" point from which the panel may be viewed—directly in front of, from either side, from close or a distance, from above or below. There are some that may have many different points of view possible and some which may be restricted to several or even one. Some may be in fact visible from any and all angles of approach. The point of view may be further complicated by such things as multiple points of view, such as sharp edges or obscuration by smaller outcropping features with in the panel itself.

These various points of view then, being taken into consideration, let us enumerate the ways in which a particular element could appear to a viewer and assume that that orientation was connected with the meaning the maker intended to convey. Right side up certainly applies more to naturalistic images than to stylized or abstract. It's opposite, up side down does the same. Might we assume, for instance that a naturalistic anthropomorph or zoomorph would be meant to convey the idea of a living animal, where as an upside down image was meant to convey a dead one; if so how does one convey wounded or sick? Vertically might be a logical answer. Variations between the two extremes may have been meant to convey other actions such as climbing, jumping, running, swimming or falling. Of course it may be that such positioning had no particular meaning at all but was instead only a function of the comfortable position in which the maker could reside while making the image or was an individual stylistic preference. It has been hypothesized by some that the orientation actually "pointed" to other glyphs, other sites, landscape features, astronomical events or alignments or to resource caches. Though not as apparent, both stylized and abstract glyphs may also have depended to some degree upon orientation for meaning. I use the word abstract as a matter of convenience, as does much of the community that studies rock art, to describe glyphs that are neither representational nor stylized but seem to be geometrically arranged with no apparent purpose. This does not mean that none is present or that the shapes have been derived from real objects, it simply means the present observer has no plausible explanation as to why they may be that shape. It is this kind of ambiguity in the field that the present discussion hopes to make some small contribution toward refining.

Certainly the orientation toward or away from other glyphs had meaning. One only need consider a series of zoomorphs for instance. If they both had antlers or horns and were facing one another and near each other, it might well be deduced that they were interacting. If a number of animal depictions appeared to be of the same species and were in a line in close proximity, it could well depict a herd moving along a well defined path. Another group in an array but all facing the same direction, particularly if behind them were other zoomorphs such as canines or anthropomorphs, maybe with weapons in hand, could well be interpreted as a group fleeing or a group in pursuit. If a group of anthropomorphs seemed to all be facing the same direction in close proximity to one another it could be deduced they were either traveling the same direction or at least looking in the same direction or at something in common.

In sites with panels facing many different directions, might the images on one of these panels have depicted corresponding frontal, side or back views of objects or the landscapes the panels faced?

Size is the next consideration when thinking about elements on a panel.

Absolute size may have a direct correlation to reality. If side by side depictions of hand prints are present and they are of different sizes, then we may deduce that what is meant is that an actual difference in size from the hands they are meant to be depicted in real life. In other cases we may not be so sure, as certainly, in some cases, exaggeration may have been used for emphasis.   One only need consider the varying degrees to which phalluses are depicted in some rock art traditions to have a clear example. Perhaps if the same image is depicted in more than one size, together they are meant to signify a relative relationship, "greater than" or "lesser than" each other.   The size of some glyphs is no doubt influenced considerably by the amount of space available on a panel, this may be further modified by about how a particular glyph maker felt about superimposing his images over those that already existed.   It is probable that some glyphs were modified because the maker simply ran out of room on the panel as we might today run out of space on the edge of a piece of paper. Where available surfaces are available, it is not uncommon to find some things, such as even large zoomorphs depicted as life size. Where a number of animals of different species are depicted, more often than not their relative real size is preserved in the petroicons.

It is possible that the size of a particular image may have been directly related to its perceived importance. In some instances pictographic scenes of gatherings of important personages are depicted as being much larger than life size. Of course in many cases, a larger image is visible from a much farther distance than a smaller one and this too may have been significant.

The size—length, height, width and depth—of the lines themselves may have also contributed to meaning. Certainly a larger expenditure of energy would have been required to make a deep definitive stroke than merely a simple scratched one and this may have related to meaning in some kind of a hierarchical way. The tendency of more definitively made lines to have more permanency, in and of itself may have embodied meaning. The superimposition of some glyphs over others, for the purpose of seeking to obliterate the lines below, modify them so their original meaning could not be ascertained or widening or deepening them to reinforce or emphasis them has obviously implied meaning.

Perspective of the image would have been an influence on meaning.   The angle at which a zoomorph's head might have been portrayed may have said a lot about the relationship between that animal and the image maker. The depiction of one large hoof of an animal would certainly mean something different than a sequence of much smaller ones of the same kind. Whether a head was depicted, realistically or stylized, the angle of depiction, head-on or in profile, may have had bearing on its exact meaning. Drawing techniques that are employed today may well have been used long ago. If one draws a group of any thing, are the ones in front of others that are drawn larger meant to convey the fact that they are closer. Is that closer meant to apply to space or might it also apply to time. If one were making a series of lines depicting a route through a landscape, the perspective would have been of tantamount   importance—was   the   space   being depicted a relatively close one, or one that may take much longer to transverse? Changing or multiple perspectives may have been depicted, perhaps giving the illusion of movement when seen from different view points.   The amount of space left between elements may also have been significant.

The depiction of details may have had influence on meaning. What information and meaning may have been compounded by the addition to digits to a stick figure, or by jewelry, hair style, accouterments or tools to more complex figures? Might "bragging rights" have been intended by conveying an antlered animal with many points.   Some traditions show internal organs realistically or stylistically, what additional meaning did that convey? Even details in abstract or stylized images, which we might normally just think of as artifacts of depiction, might have meaning for the person who made them. In a stylized animal depiction of a mask there may be a series of dots, to us just part of the decoration—for the maker of the dots though, perhaps a depiction of the number of such animals he had killed. When we talked about the placement of lines above, we have already discussed how small details may have influenced meaning in ways that are quite difficult for us to grasp these days. Or perhaps not, we have only to consider the difference between the meaning of a small cross bar placed on a vertical line that makes it a "t" instead of an "l" in our western alphabet. Some minor details may simply be due to variation in tools used or the condition of the rock surface itself and may have no meaning at all.

While connection of glyphs by touching may certainly at times be incidental or unintentional, there are others when that connectedness may be directly related to the meaning of both symbols. This may be true of glyphs made in different time periods as well as ones made contemporaneously at the same panel. Let us suppose that we knew that our grandfather had made an image of an animal and that he had a ritual of coming and refurbishing that glyph before going on each hunt and that he was always a successful hunter. You came to know this because your father had passed this ritual and its practice on to you. Each time you and your father revisited and renewed that glyph you were making a connection. Over many generations, the original glyph may have been completely obliterated but the place and act of making it was still important so that the glyph now was a ritual rather than an actual making of an image. Let us imagine at some time during that long period you or your son decided that as well as using the magic to hunt sheep, he would also like to use it to hunt deer—he might modify the image to reflect that new understanding and utilization.

By depicting two images touching one another perhaps the idea of close relationship or even ownership may have been depicted. Or achievements such as counting coup or killing of enemies may have been portrayed.   Anthropomorphs stabbing spears into zoomorphs unequivocally depict a relationship— as we shall see later, determining the exact nature of that relationship is more difficult than it seems on the surface. The combining of many elements on a single panel may be intended to express a sequence of events such as those of a battle. Such a depiction would not tell of the events in a linear fashion, but rather depict them all at once, perhaps serving as a mnemonic device to prompt views to remember the sequence of events and be able to recount them.

The combination of several images into a single connected one may be a way of depicting such things as names that combine many elements. When they have been combined they may overlap or appear to be highly stylized or even abstract. This effect may be compounded if they are used over a period of time in a variety of places. And some may undergo a continual process of permutation as they continue to be used. In some more advanced glyph systems, such as the Mayan glyphs, such combinations may occur in layers leaving only some elements from underlying elements visible in subsequent ones.

Repetition is another factor of relatedness between elements on a single panel. The very nature of petroglyphs in particular lends itself to the repetition of elements, particularly abstract ones such as lines and dots. Such marks readily bring to mind counting and tallying and most of us can not imagine a world in which such activities would not be useful. The excess of these at some sites though leaves us

99

wondering about what could those who left them been counting. Perhaps some such marks are nothing more than idle, incidental, time filling exercises such as doodling.   Others may have been made as "practice" to learn how to coordinate eye hand movements so that the making of other more complex images might be produced. Perhaps they were just simple things done to teach children how to concentrate and to improve their eye/hand coordination.

Almost certainly in many cases, repetition of images were meant to convey patterns or cycles such as the phases of the moon or equinoxes or solstices. The depiction of many images of the same thing may have been meant to imply abundance or hope for abundance. Or certain symbols either naturalistic, stylized or abstract may have been symbols representing desirable things or occurrences and the repeated manufacture of them was thought to insure their continued or return supply. There are some who believe the depiction of big horn sheep in the American Great Basin tradition represents the results of shamanistic rituals involving the insuring continuation of the weather phenomena of rain.

A simple aesthetic sense on the part of the individual making the glyph may have resulted in symmetry being present. Even some simple abstract designs such as wavy lines evoke a degree of symmetry and that may have been recognized and enhanced by the creators. To make mirror images from one side to the other would have been integral to the drawing of such images as circles. The ability to do that may have been perceived of as having great power by those not knowing the mechanism where by it was accomplished.   Might not then, the production of asymmetrical images be attempts to disrupt or demonstrate the opposite of what ever the symmetrical may have meant?   It may be that depictions of symmetry were recognition of the idea of balance which seems to exist throughout nature. By making symmetrical images it may have been believed by some that that balance would be perpetuated.   Or perhaps the basic duality found throughout nature and subsequently language was being depicted.

We have examined the various considerations of how petroicons were produced. We have seen that during each facet the makers had choices from many options. Each of those choices would have been opportunity to associate meaning with a particular glyph or group of glyphs.

CHAPTER FIVE

WHAT WAS DEPICTED BY ROCK ART?

What is depicted by markings on stone that are collectively called rock art? As I have stated earlier, even the term "art" is somewhat of a misnomer, and I choose to sometimes refer to the markings as petroicons. For most researchers this distinction has been resolved; I am among the few who still use the term. To me, it is just more accurate and this is not the place to reiterate the pros and cons of such usage.

We may begin this facet of our discussion about what those petroicons depict by making a distinction between marks that were intentionally made and those that were left unintentionally or as artifacts of other processes. This seems necessary because in some cases the difference between the two is difficult to discern. It is not meant to imply that all grooves, circles and pits are unintentionally made, there are some rock art locations, such as in the British Isles, where such markings were quite intentionally produced over considerable areas and ranges of time.

Stone tools, by their very nature, require frequent reworking in order to hold their shape and/or their edges. While other portable stones may frequently have been used for that process, stones that were much larger and consequently not movable were also employed. That may, in some cases, been due to the fact they were made of stone that was harder than the tools and at others simply because they were located in a convenient place near where the tools were being used. Tool sharpening marks are found as a results of Neolithic Era tools being reworked but much more frequently after the age of metals began. After the advent of the metal plow, marks were made on many stones as a result of the use of this implement. In some cases larger stones themselves may have been modified to serve as tools. An example of this is stones along major rivers that have been modified to facilitate the removal of fish oil, or others near the drip line of caves that were modified to channel water away from the cave interior. In places where some food resources had shells or tough husks and it was necessary to hold them stationary so the edible portion could be accessed, multiple holes were made in horizontal rock faces for this purpose.

Some stones have mineral properties that may have made them useful for dietary reasons or because the substance of the stone was thought to have medicinal or magical properties.   Stones in tidal areas for instance, may have accumulated salt in vugs and cracks and this substance was valued. One method of, so to speak, harvesting such resources was to drill into them with harder stones and extract the resulting powder. This process would leave behind cupules which are frequently cited as being part of the rock art legacy. These cupules may, in some cases, be the results of enlarging natural vugs in the stone. There is evidence that such man made depressions were sometimes associated with fertility practices, such as repositories for umbilical cord stumps. If the site were associated with birth or death, portions of the stone, sometimes in powder form were removed for use in ritual or talismanic magic. Weather control was another practice that sometimes involved making marks on stone. Rain particularly was "caused" to fall by the drilling of holes in rocks, and the subsequent covering of such holes was believed to make it cease. The powder that was extracted from some particular types of rock may have been used as a grit in the processing of other stones or as a polishing powder. These simple holes, no matter what the reason they were produced, have frequently been modified by connecting lines or lines that highlighted them by encircling them. It is possible that some shapes made while obtaining the powder increased its potency. Some depressions in stones and perhaps "spirals" may have been early parts of the process of creating utilitarian artifacts such as mortars and would cease to exist when the artifact was fully created.

It is important that marks created by these processes be recognized, but also important to reason that their meaning stay very closely associated with the reason for their existence. Their meaning was their purpose.   Intentionally produced marks on stone, as we are about to see, lend themselves to a much broader range of meaningful interpretation.

We may classify marks intentionally made on stone by three categories: naturalistic, stylized or abstract. We can further delineate them from one another as being signs, emblems or symbols. Each of these divisions is an opportunity for meaning to be associated with the petroicons. It is important that we remember that these terms are simply a convenient way of referring to them and that analogies that result may not necessarily have valid real life correspondences. For instance, two circles connected by a line may resemble what we call a barbell today, and we may refer to it as a barbell motif, when in fact we know that when such glyphs were made throughout the American Great Basin, no such physical object existed.   As well as being generated by actual objects, objects that appeared in dream or trance states may have been additional sources of inspiration for glyphs. Such imagery may combine real life elements into imaginary constructs. For example, the form of a hatchet may be combined with that of a large beaked bird and be depicted as growing from a leaved plant form. Relationships between the images, their subject matter and their meaning in the social context in which they are generated are all factors that must be examined. By examining what was depicted, we may then conjecture about what the depictions meant to the makers. As we shall see, there are many ways, both simple and complex, in which we can approach even images that seem to be the same thing that imbue them with different meanings. Perhaps the following discussion will illuminate some of the ways in which we can begin to distinguish the similarities and differences that will aid in that undertaking.

Naturalistic glyphs are those whose shape resembles real world objects. These may be defined as anthropomorphs, zoomorphs and plant forms. The ratio in which these types of naturalistic glyphs occur may denote a factor of the relative importance these things had to the glyph makers.

Anthropomorphs are depictions of human beings. These range from very simplistic often incomplete "stick figure" drawings to complex more realistic depictions including details of hair and ear decorations, clothing, other accouterments and the depiction of weapon and tool use. Physiological details such as toes, fingers and sexual organs may be shown, although these tend to be depicted in generic ways rather than as depicting actual configurations. Stylized anthropomorphic rock art includes such things as depictions of obviously human foot and

107

hand prints, faces or facial features and silhouettes and phallic or vulva forms. Or they may be more mask like rather than realistic with fanciful decorations and other imaginative details added, although they are still recognizable as representing humans.

Zoomorphs are depictions of animals. These range from realistic simple stick figures and outlines to more complex depictions with such things as skin markings or decorative patterns visible. Details such as horns, antlers or rattles on snakes may be present. A wide range of animal species are depicted, ranging from mammals to reptiles and amphibians to birds and insects. Various poses such as running or jumping may be depicted. Occasionally, copulating animals and birth scenes are present. More stylized representations include such thing as pelts, paw prints, hoof prints, horns or antlers depicted alone and teeth or claws.

A combination of anthroporphic and zoomorphic characteristics are found in some glyphs. Such depictions are called theriomorphs. These frequently combine more stylistic elements that are often greatly exaggerated, rather than realistic ones. Such combinations can lead some to interpret them as depicting "gods" or other "spirit" creatures or mythological monsters.

Petrosomatoglyphs are considered by some to belong to the rock art tradition. These are images of parts of human or animal bodies, such as foot and hand prints, that are usually incised quite deeply into stones. There are often myths defining who made them or for what purpose, that survive to present day. Standing in or touching such depressions is sometimes thought to impart useful benefits to the participant. In some cases the indentation is used as a bowel containing liquids with absolutional or curative properties.

Plant forms that are depicted as rock art range from very simple outlines of general morphology to more detailed representations of flowers and seed pods. Parts of plants such as flowers, seeds or cones may be depicted rather than the entire plant. These may be quite realistic or very stylized, the later being often mistaken for abstract imagery. Modifiers on plant form images may have indicated that it was edible, poison or that it had special properties such as being psychoactive when ingested or otherwise utilized. The properties of some of these plants are experienced when their smoke is inhaled. The juices of certain plants is utilized by the application to the skin, as in the case of aloe vera being used as a treatment for burns. These methods of utilization may have been depicted in association with plant form glyphs.

Petroicons whose shapes have no readily discernible corollary in the real world as abstract. These may take a large variety of forms ranging from very simple to highly complex. For classification purposes, these are referred to by some as rectilinear or curvilinear compositions.   Rectilinear forms tending to be straight lines with well defined geometrically shaped corners, while curvilinear lines are more curved or rounded. Simple dots, lines and circles are commonly found through the corpus of world wide rock art. Combinations of these and other basic geometrical forms such as squares and triangles are often found,   either alone or in combination. Complex patterns may extend over large areas of panels and in some cases cover the entire surface of the stones. The lines of which they are composed may be separated quite distinctly from one another or may be intricately interwoven into an overall design. It is well to take note that some things that now appear to us as abstract may have in fact been representative of real life. A good example of this would be a map or a mnemonic device to show someone a trail and points of reference along the way. Illustration of the course of a water way would also appear to be quite abstract. It may be that some very meticulously repeated patterns, particularly when in close proximity to one another may have been nothing more than a glyph maker exhibiting his prowess and ability to control his tools. Some lines seem to have been made as borders or frames for other glyphs, perhaps to call more attention to them or to separate from other glyphs on the same panel.   Along the same lines (and admittedly, this idea is a long stretch,) perhaps there were contests engaged in out of boredom, whose outcome was determined by who could make the longest, biggest, visible the most far away or some other criteria, glyph. Perhaps games were indulged in and many lines and dots were simply ways of keeping score. Since lifetimes in general were shorter then than now, might we assume that the playful childish mind may have persisted longer than it does today? Perhaps some patterns were made simply to "decorate" the surroundings or to make the setting more interesting. Perhaps in some cases, a picture was just that, a picture—rock art in a true sense of the phrase. It is not inconceivable that some imagery may have been produced for duplicitous reasons, perhaps to give the impression that someone else had been there, when in fact they hadn't or to mislead someone whose following may not have been welcome. It has been suggested by some that a small group of often occurring images may be the results of the physiological phenomena of phosphines and entoptic imagery. The first is imagery that appears in the eye without the presence of light, such as when the surface of the eyeball is pressed with eyes closed. The second is imagery that may appear when light passes through certain structures, such as blood vessels, in the eye itself while the lids are closed. These form constants, as they are called, may be in the form of honeycomb like lattices, checkerboards, triangles, cobwebs, tunnels and spirals. The occurrence of both may be caused or intensified by the ingestion of certain psychoactive drugs such as mescaline or by more natural stimuli such as sleep deprivation, illness, prolonged periods of being in darkness or fasting. After imagery, caused by such things as looking at the setting sun and then blinking may have been yet another cause of some imagery that people attempted to project onto the surface of stone. In some traditions a visual image called a mandala is used as meditative device, such an image may appear to one unfamiliar with the concept as a composition that is a combination of rectilinear and curvilinear lines.

Between realistic and abstract, we have some glyphs that may be called stylized. These are images that, through exaggeration of some parts and/or the omission of others still are meant to represent something. Often distortions in prominence and size of parts of what is depicted make the origin of the image nearly unrecognizable. Faces for instance, may become mask like with extreme emphasis on eyes and mouth. A more modern example may be found in the *fleur de lis* which represents a lily.

Another convenient way in which we can examine what is depicted by petroicons is by their purpose. This may be done with greater or lesser ease and there is certainly the element of overlapping interpretations for any given glyph or group of glyphs. Some glyphs are symbols, others signs and others emblems. All may be represented by the types just discussed.

Symbols are visual images with universally understood meanings over broad areas.   That universality may be among subsets within the area such as a particular tribe, group, group of groups or like believing individuals.

Signs are visual images that impart a directive idea such as pointing to a particular feature or in the case of astronomical observations, phenomena. They might also be indicative of such things as directions for travel or of warnings for such occurrences as flash floods.

Emblems are visual images that represent such things as a group, boundaries or an individual identity.

Other considerations when we think about what was depicted in rock art are origin, number, size and proportion. We shall examine those in detail below.

In some cases, certainly the image may have been absolutely unique and original to the person making it—a one of a kind, so to speak. It may be argued that any images made by a different person or even images made by the same person are unique. In dealing with the actual mechanics and techniques to execute the drawing that would be valid—different brushes, pigments, locations and surfaces are certainly used. However, when discussing the actual subject matter of the glyph, or its shape in the case of abstracts, relatively few images can be considered unique. And although the particular image was one of a kind, chances are it incorporated elements that occur else where in its most basic design. This singular uniqueness increases with the complexity of the design it self, as may also the amount of "borrowed" characteristics.

Images that are copies of others in subject matter are much more common. Perhaps most were not true copies, but only some one else depicting the same thing. And it may be there are universal ways in which simple things like humans are depicted by the inexperienced or young makers—stick figures come to mind. The depicted shape of some objects were doubtlessly culturally defined, the shape used to depict an animal pelt in one group may have been quite different in that of another. Copies may have been produced by children copying the work of their

114

elders. Copies may have been made of previously existing images just for the exercise of proving to oneself one could do it, or do it better than the original. This process may have taken place with out much thought as to why one would think this a necessary exercise. Or if the imagery were deemed important for some reason, it may have been copied to perpetuate or reproduce results thought to have been generated by the production of the original. This may have been done at the same, or nearly the same time, or over much longer periods of time, even perhaps transgenerationally. Over the course of time the meaning of such renewal may have been lost and its repetition simply become part of the institutionalized ritual associated with a particular site, panel or element.

The number of times an image is repeated at a site, particularly by the original maker or makers of the panel, may have had several different significances. If an image were powerful enough by its recognition then a single instance of it might well serve the intention of the maker at the time of its manufacture and in the future. It might signify a single instance of the object depicted, such as the killing of a particularly large game animal. If a single image appears a number of times then it may be simply depicting the plural, the idea of more than one; this could have been a way of generically expressing that idea or plurality or have been an actual account, as in "we killed six deer here today." If a number of animals were depicted in a line, it may have simply indicated that a herd was seen passing by from that location. If such images were added to the same site over time, then similar ideas may have been being expressed but with the added temporal element. If many images were made of the same animal at the same site over a long period of time perhaps it conveyed the idea that anyone visiting the site might be very likely to see the same animal. Of course the meaning of the actual creature may change with the passing of time. As a hypothetical example, let us use the depiction of a large rattlesnake. Perhaps the original image was made because someone was bitten by one at that location and died. Another snake may have been added later as a warning to those who approached the site that there was a rattlesnake den there and subsequently danger.   Let us further suppose that at a time distant from that, people approached who were starving to death because of drought. To them the sign of the presence of a rattlesnake may have meant a meal was nearby. Further removed in time perhaps a medicine person came upon the image and knew they could find the venom there that was used for its curative properties. At another time, those who had in common the habit of consuming snake meat may have been known collectively as the "snake eaters" and when they came upon the glyph they would have surmised that members of their group had been there previously.

The size of the element may also have had a bearing on the intent of the maker. Its relative size on the panel, or in relation to other glyphs, may have indicated its perceived relative importance to the maker. That may or may not have been shared by those viewing it. Size may have been a function of the distance from which the image was intended to be viewed; obviously, the larger the image, in some settings at least, the farther away it could be seen. If two images of the same thing are present and they are of different sizes, it may have been meant to show the difference in their actual size. Depending upon the object itself, a maker of a petroicon would have three choices—showing it life size, showing it smaller than life size or showing it larger than life size. Each of these choices could have projected a different meaning. On occasion, a figure, human or animal appears to have an extra digit or appendage. There are several reasons this may appear. It may be a simple result of an inept tool application, a reflection of real people who were born with extra fingers or toes, a distorted perception, perhaps an attempt to reflect real life when one places ones feet close together, or it may have just been made to call attention to it or its dramatic effect and shock value

117

as being something out of the ordinary. Physiological anomalies were certainly observable in the animal world as well.

In some cases the size of the glyph is certainly influenced greatly simply by the size of the space available on which to place it. This limitation may be dictated by the physical properties of the rock itself, edges, corners or niches or by a desire on the part of the maker to not infringe on the space already occupied by other glyphs. As panels age, especially ones that are in continual usage over long periods of time, there is a tendency for less and less attention to be paid to superimposition considerations. The size may also have been a function of how long a particular glyph would take to produce and the amount of time available to the maker. Another consideration that we might loosely associate with size, is degree of completeness. There are innumerable cases no doubt where the process may have been interrupted by pressing matters of survival such as warding off predators or poisonous critters or movement away from the site toward the next exploitable resource such as ripening berries or roots mature enough for harvest.

The proportionality of an image would have presented another series of choices for the producer. To show things in correct relative proportion would have made them the most life like if that were the

118

intention. If perspective was trying to be illustrated, images that were closer may have been made larger and those more distant smaller. Exaggeration of proportion may have been a function of the technological competence of the maker or it may have served to emphasis the perceived importance of certain elements. Anthropomorphs with exaggerated genitalia depictions are found nearly universally. Although it seems like bragging rights, "my what ever is bigger or better or whatever than yours" is a modern phenomenon, we have little reason to believe it may not have existed in past times as well. We can not discount the fact that since even today things are often drawn out of proportion for their humorous value, that may not have been a motivation in the past. Exaggeration may have also been used to depict perceived abilities, characteristics or attributes. A leader for instance may have been depicted with a much larger headdress that was unrealistically proportional to his body. Culturally dictated conventions may have also been the reason for some exaggerations. For instance, our people wear very nicely crafted moccasins made of animal hides and the neighbors were simple woven sandals so when we depict our people we will make their feet elongated and elliptical.

This facet of our discussion has shown us how what first appears to be a great many different subjects in rock art, may in fact be distilled into a manageable number of variations on basic themes. It is the smaller variations incorporated in those basics that imbue individual glyphs with their purposes and meanings.

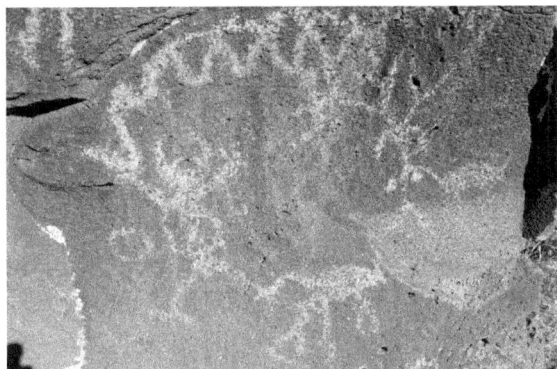

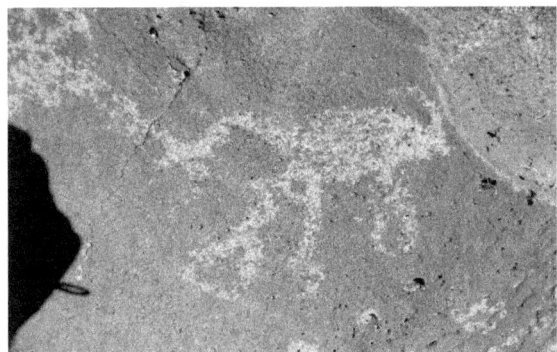

121

CHAPTER SIX

WHY WAS ROCK ART MADE?

With the issues of who, what, how, and when discussed in detail, we can now turn our attention to the question of why rock art was made. When all five of these areas of attention are considered in regard to a particular example of rock art, we can be closer to arriving at an understanding of its purpose and meaning. Some of the following points have been touched on in the previous discussions, this is inevitable during such a detailed examination of a subject. It is hoped that the reader will allow endure the indulgence of such repetition. While I have attempted to give several examples of each reason, the reader can perhaps come up with as many more that would serve as well.

There are many words that may be used to describe the distinction that I will make in the conclusion of this paragraph; they each require many qualifications and nuances of definition. None the less, I have chosen to divide rock art into two categories when discussing why it was made. The first is nonverbal and the second verbal.

Nonverbal glyphs are those that express an idea that may be understood without the process of spoken or written language being involved.   We may categorize these in the following way. Please note this list is not intended to convey any kind of a hierarchy of meaning or importance by its order.

ADVISORY marks serve a great many purposes. They may warn of hidden dangers such as flash floods or danger from animals such as snakes. They may be directional markers, indicating the correct path, a path that was taken or the reverse of both of these. They could be combined with mathematical marks to indicate number of days travel between points. Some marks may have served as judgment indications and notices about conditions and suitability for places for purposes such as camping. Lines or scratches across others may have served to negate or nullify previously indicated information, or, as is the case today with the ubiquitous circle with a diagonal line through it, to prohibit some behavior.

LOCATIONAL marks may indicate the presence of food or other resources or indicate where caches of such things may be located. Marks may indicate a view of a landscape, a map, with features such as waterways, mountains, features on the horizon and other landmarks indicated. To be comprehensible to those referring to them, an understanding of scale and orientation would have been required and marks indicating these may have been included. Such maps may have been used to indicate seasonal rounds, locations of friends and enemies, migration routes or have been guides for safe passage through wetlands or mountain passes. They may have been made with explicit details, showing bends and corners in water courses or trails; have shown only approximate relationships between features such as landmarks or geologically unique features; or quite general, perhaps only indicating that a trail goes right or left for some distance. In some cases the intended movement of small groups such as families may have been made so that when relatives came looking for them they would be able to be found. In some cases where large pieces of territory might be divided, such as might result from a treaty among warring parties, a map may have been used to delimit such agreements. Perhaps smaller maps might be used to show the division of arable land among a number of families or to plot the efficient planting or rotation of crops. It is not inconceivable that in societies that had beliefs about underworlds and life after death, that maps might have been drawn to aid in navigation there as well. In some parts of the world, the entrance to the underworld was thought to have been the cracks in rocks or caves and some glyphs may be reinforcing the location of these places that were perceived as being portals. In landscapes marks on stone may have indicated pathways through marginally navigable passages such as mountain passes. Marks on stone may have served a purpose during explorations of unknown areas; one might leave behind marks for others who were following that indicated a direction of travel and for how long, a turn right or left and travel for how long and perhaps anticipated return to the starting point. Scarcity of water along certain routes, or   last chances to refurbish water supplies would have been important information left behind by markings on stone.

IDENTIFYING marks could be either of a personal or collective nature. Individuals may have developed a series of marks they could make on stones that indicated their unique identity, much as our signatures do today.   Such marks may have included status indicators, such as elaborate head dresses or more abstract markings, such as rays emanating from the head or other parts of the body. Groups, small and large, may have been identified by glyphs of a heraldic nature, perhaps indicating such things as predominate food resources upon which the group was dependent or animals unique to the areas they inhabited. In such areas, boundaries may have been recognized and marked with identifying marks of those who claimed them. In societies with identifiable deities, these names too were probably represented by marks on stone. We know that early Christians used the icthys, a stylized representation of a fish, to represent their affiliation. Of course many of these deities, in time, became represented in three dimensional sculptures, but depiction in two dimensions on stone probably preceded those. There are some food plants, such as camas, whose usefulness could only be determined by the color of the blooms (bulbs with the wrong color blooms are poisonous.) In some places where identification could not take place until that stage of growth, there may have been signs left on stones indicating the eventual usefulness or not of the plants growing there.

MATHEMATICAL marks such as tally marks or geometrical constructs would not only often have had meaning of their own, but may have also served as modifiers as in the case of exploration cited above. Simple counting and tallying would have made many tasks, such as the dividing of plentiful resources or keeping track of volume of harvests, more manageable. Measuring things would also have been facilitated by the making of marks on stone. One only has to call to mind how, in many families today, a record of children's heights as they grow is marked with subsequent lines on a wall. Keeping track of cycles of various kinds would have been aided by series of dots or lines. It is not unreasonable to assume that lunar and menstrual cycles may have been subject to such recording. In agrarian societies especially, keeping track of solar cycles by recording of equinoxes and solstices would have been important. Recording of such cycles eventually lead to calendar systems which may have been preserved on stone as well. Geometrical arrangements, patterns and lengths for such things as strands of baskets, nets or textiles may have been illustrated for teaching or replication purposes.

INSTRUCTIONAL marks would have had many uses such as those mentioned directly above. Simple templates may have been used as descriptive sample devices for teaching those just learning a skill such as basket making; more complicated ones may have been made to aide in remembering how to construct more complex patterns. A sequence of glyphs may have been used to record the series of actions necessary to successfully accomplish complex tasks such as curing animal pelts. Perhaps strategies for battles to be fought or hunting patterns were explained by leaders to large groups by making markings on stone illustrating positions and movements. Other complex tasks such as the construction of fish weirs may have, on occasion, necessitated the use of illustrations for successful completion. This may have been particularly crucial if a large number of people were involved in the activity. It may be argued that most of these endeavors were probably accomplished with simple verbal direction and example, and that is no doubt a valid point, however, if one examines many activities of groups today that are managed by design, drawings such as blue prints are essential to success. Or, simple clues such as marks that identified what kind of bait was likely to catch the most fish at any given place, would have had a useful role in day to day activity. Other marks may have been incidental to training in eye/ hand coordination, practice in the motions on materials of lesser value before actually using more scarce or valuable ones. The process of knapping or shaping tools by repeatedly striking a stone in a very precise manner must have been a skill acquired through practice, perhaps accounting for the widespread appearance of what would seem to be random dot patterns.

MNEMONIC marks served as reminders, in all probability, not only for the makers, but at times for others. The time period over which such marks were meant to function probably varied considerably. In some cases they may have served to mark a path through unfamiliar territory through which the maker intended to return in the near or distant future. At others, such as grave markers, they may have served as reminders over many generations. In hunter gatherer societies that moved through wide territories in yearly rounds for the purpose of exploiting seasonal resources, marks may have been left to remind those returning of important details such as, perhaps, where to dig for underground water. This would have great benefit if members of the group who had been there before were unable to go in subsequent years because of illness, death or some other grave circumstance.

DECORATIVE marks may have been made on stones for much the same purpose as decorations are used today—to reinforce the stability of the familiar leading to feelings of comfort. Dwellings in many different locations are made of stone and earth and would have provided ready surfaces for such petroicons. In some cases entire surfaces may have been covered with designs, while at others a single image or two would have served the purpose, much as hung pictures, tiles and wall paper does today. Decorative motifs may have shared commonality with designs used in pottery making, basket weaving, fabric design and body ornamentation traditions. In some cases decorative marks may have incorporated the meaning of ownership or the identity of the person constructing the edifice. Decorations of various designs may have reinforced elements of ritual in locations that were used for such purposes. Some petroicons were probably thought to express power for such things as protection from malevolent forces and would have been a prominent part of some decorative environments.

RECORDING marks served a broad range of purposes for both the unusual and the familiar. As discussed in locational marks above, one purpose would have been to record people's movements through landscapes. To leave an account of being witness to an event may have inspired other petroicons to be made. Events such as successful hunts, accidental drownings or other traumatic events, landslides, feats of heroic proportion or skill, widespread illnesses like small pox or devastating famine may have all been subjects deemed worth recording. Unique, one of a kind, previously unknown or rarely occurring experiences such as stars going supernova, eclipses of the sun and moon, the eruption of volcanoes, the arrival of new people by ship or some other means or ship wrecks would all provide subject matter. To imagine how this might have served as inspiration, we have only to look at how such events today send many people scrambling for their cameras.

ACOUSTICAL marks may have been made simply by virtue of the fact that some stones, when struck by others, produce "ringing" sounds of various qualities. The sound of stone hitting stone by one or more people simultaneously may have aroused the curiosity of some types of animals inducing them to approach where they might be more easily harvested. It may have served the purpose of disturbing others to the point where they might leave their burrows or hiding places and thus become easier prey to hunters.

131

It seems unlikely that a formal system of musical notation would have been present in the archaic rock art record, still, the possibility of cruder precursors can not be dismissed. Today, there are diagrams that illustrate the steps of various dances; might not such diagrams have been used as instructional tools in the past as well? Many locations where rock art is found have configurations of stone or landscape that make them particularly suited for the production of echoes. Marks may have been made on stone to call attention to this fact or to demonstrate that property.

NONSENSICAL marks may have been made that way by the makers or simply understood that way by those later trying to interpret them. Marks that appear to be random and without form, what are commonly referred to a graffiti, may have at the time represented something to the maker. Or they may not have, they may have been made as mindlessly as we might make doodles on a pad of paper while engaged in a telephone call. It may be that some where produced as a simple release of individual tension, much as some might even today pound on a wall or table in an attempt to do the same thing. Others may have been made as a joke or a cartoon or a pun or a parody, the meaning of which may have been very short lived or only have been comprehensible to the one toward whom it was directed. Others may have been made as part of games, some perhaps involving

132

the imagined shapes made by the interaction of shade and light. Games such as modern hop-scotch require some sort of drawing on the surface upon which the game is played, precursors or games that have long been forgotten, may have required similar props to be played.

FUNCTIONAL marks may be artifacts left behind by the purpose for which the rock surface was used. These would include serrated edges used in the process of extracting oil from fish or the removal of flesh from hides; pits for holding nuts or seeds while they were being separated from their husks or shells; crevices for holding shell fish while their meat was being extracted; pits with channels adjacent for the extraction and collection of animal blood or juices from fruits. Tools such as ground stone mortars, in the very earliest moments of their manufacture may have simply been scratches or spirals to define the area to be removed.   If such a process were interrupted and never resumed, those marks would remain. Removal of spalls for the manufacture of Neolithic tools would have left marks of percussion in many cases. This may appear to be a deliberate pattern to a later observer, particularly if this occurred a great many times over a long period of time at the same place. This phenomena could also result if the stone itself were being harvested for its perceived curative or magical powers. In some cases like in the case of baby rocks or rain rocks where a series of pits is present, it was the function of the holes themselves that was important, not their appearance. When, for instance, rain was desired, many cupules may have been filled with water.

COMEMORATIVE marks were made to evoke memories of a particular person or event. The most obvious of these is the recording of deaths, either by direct marking of graves, or by creating images of the deceased. We can imagine that, among peoples who used identifying marks for individual purposes, that same glyph may have been used to mark the place in which their remains were interred. Portraits of a series of leaders may have been made to commemorate the period of time over which each held influence in an attempt to convey a sense of continuity. The perceived importance of each leader or their attributes may have embellished the actual portrayal itself. Other lineages and genealogical information may have been portrayed, especially if there was a definite beginning point of a group or family history in a place, such as the arrival from distant land by boat. Important celebrations and treaties or alliances were commemorated by the making of marks on stone so their place, time and import would not soon be forgotten.

EVOCATIVE marks were made by those who believed that through those marks desired out comes could be invoked or undesired ones avoided. This may have been as simple as a "welcome" sign over an entrance way or a series of marks that were part of a complex ritual. Some of these may have been produced by ordinary members of societies, although they were probably more frequently made by the healers, medicine people or shamans. The later, particularly would have used such signs in the application of sympathetic magic. This has been discussed in detail earlier. As well as the actual image of the marks, other rituals such as repeating, touching or smelling of them may have also played some part in their perceived power. These marks may have been made for the purpose of gaining control over such relatively trivial things as the curing of a cough or larger scale ambitions such as the changing of weather or climate patterns. Youths, and some times adults, in certain cultures are known to have employed vision or spirit quests as a means of discovering or reinforcing certain personality traits and "powers." During such quests, petroicons were sometimes produced as either aids in producing visions or in recording such visions after they had occurred. Repetition or renewal of such images may have been believed to increase or prolong the strength of such visions. Some times such evocative marks would have served as envoys as demonstrated by natives who made petroicons where they would be repeatedly covered and exposed by tides, carrying the message of "welcome" or "please return" to fish or other animals who lived in the sea.

This discussion about the meaning of rock art, as was explained in the beginning, has placed the limit on what is being included for consideration as marks on stone that predate writing. We have just seen that there are many forms of petroiconography that are not dependent upon language for their meaning to be conveyed. Now let us turn to marks on stone whose interpretation may have been dependent on interpretation with language.

A small side note before we begin however. There are some who believe that certain rock art conventions may have been mirrors for unspoken sign languages that were often understood by a variety of people who had no spoken language in common. This theory is worth considering but so far seems unsupported except by a very small sampling from a single tradition. Even unsubstantiated, it still holds some appeal, as sign language has surely been part of the human communication repertoire for a very long time. This theory seems to fall between the two broad categories under discussion here, hence its mention.

If we are going to posit that the meanings of some markings on stone were meant to convey a verbal meaning, then it is important to remind ourselves that there are many fashions of speaking. These range through a spectrum from baby talk, songs, incantations, day to day conversation, swearing, demanding, admonishing, correcting, instructing, boasting, swearing, speech making and whispers. Any interpretation of lingual glyphs may need to take the intended tone and state of mind of the maker into account.

It is generally held that for every word there is an idea and vise versa. It is reasonable to believe that, before alphabets and other lexigraphic systems of writing developed, there were ways in which ideas could be expressed. At its most basic, and this is largely simplified, language is a noun and a verb. Regardless of the syntax, these are the two root elements. They may be elaborated on in any number of ways, from verb tense to modifiers such as adjectives and adverbs. Let us confine our discussion to these basics and see how those may have been represented by marks on stone. While it is fairly easy to see how a picture of something can depict it as a real life object, a noun, it is more difficult to imagine how a stationary two dimensional mark may represent an action or a state of being, a verb. Perhaps the easiest way to do this is by presenting examples and imagining how we might go about expressing language through them.

This idea is predicated on the idea that rock art represents equivocal ideas in speech. This is almost surely the case, but, if it isn't then what are the alternatives? Do visual ideas exist previously? Even if they do, they still have an objective correlative, something causes the verbal reaction and its modification into language. Intrinsically, certain sounds have a definitive meaning; a grunt or cry made as a result of being in pain is recognized nearly universally. Repetition of the same sound under the same or similar circumstances leads to the recognition of meaning—the magic moment when sound made by a human serves to convey meaning. It may have been those rudimentary "words" that humans attempted to convey with their markings on stone. It makes little sense that given the medium, a mark maker would suddenly make up nonsensical sounds to record, it is much more likely that they would seek a way of conveying self made meaningful sounds so that the marks would convey that meaning to others.

Now let us make an example. Let us draw a realistic four legged animal with an enclosed body area. Let us draw an abstract circle. Call the animal, "food." Call the circle, "me." Separately, we have two nouns. Now let us draw an animal with a circle around it; now we have food surrounded by me, or in other words, "I food inside" or "I eat." Now let us

138

draw two concentric circles, that gives us more than one "I" put the circles around the animal and "we eat" results. Perhaps, instead of drawing concentric circles we simply drew a bigger circle to indicate a larger group of people.   Circles around say a quadruped and a lizard, following this line of reasoning, would mean, "We eat more than one kind of food." In dealing with number, further modifications could be added to indicate more. These may be individually indicated by tally marks or dots nearby or by some other marks, perhaps circle fragments or hoof prints, that might not be the same as the original sign. I add antlers or horns to the quadruped and now I have distinguished it as being either a deer or an antelope, or perhaps a male or female (the later perhaps pregnant by drawing a smaller zoomorph inside the body outline), or perhaps a young (by drawing spots inside the body area) or mature specimen. Now let me draw two circles a short distance apart and connect them with a straight line. I have now duplicated the symbol for "I" and moved it to another location, perhaps indicating "I move." Now place an animal figure inside one of the circles and the glyph now indicates "I move to eat." But wait, I didn't eat the food on the hoof, I had to kill it first, so I draw a stick figure that now represents "I" with a bow and arrow in its hands which indicate "hunt", or I draw the animal with an

arrow in its side and as a result have "I kill animal."
Now let us imagine that I am hungry and there are no
animals in sight, there are however, petroicons of
animals nearby with arrows in some of them. Those
images "speak to me" and tell me "this is a place
where animals were killed." A while later there are
still no animals in sight and I am getting hungrier so I
make a stone marking that resembles an animal and
put an arrow in its side, saying to myself "I wish this
animal were here so I could kill it." And at the same
time I am thinking that the animal can hear me
calling it to me by making its image. A day later I
am really, really hungry and still no animal has come
to this place, so I decide that I must go else where to
hunt it. However, I can see that the distance I will
probably need to go is quiet far and I am expecting
the arrival of the rest of my group at the same site in
a couple of days. They will want to know where I
have gone. So I draw two circles a distance apart
with a line in between them, this time being careful to
position the second circle so that it indicates the
direction in which I intend to travel. I put an animal
inside the second circle. I put a small zigzag line in
front of the second circle because I can see some
sharp peaks on the horizon in the direction that I am
going to travel. I anticipate that I will travel four
days, so across the connecting line between the
circles I make four smaller circles to indicate the

140

number of days I intend to travel in that direction. So the expression to the arriving family after looking at all the glyphs is "I am hungry and no food is here so I went four days toward the mountains to look for it."

We can see from this imaginary example that both abstract and representative glyph may have been used as subject and verbs with modifications of various sorts that would have made them capable of conveying quite complex ideas and series of ideas not only in the present tense but over time. Many of these modifications in all likelihood were conventions understood by many people over wide areas since they appear quite widely distributed in some area rock art surveys and inventories. However it is also likely there were signs that were only understood among small self selected groups or individuals. As language is a dialog of opposites, it is reasonable to suppose that many glyphs had either individual glyphs that stood for their opposites, or modifications that indicated the opposite was meant. Glyphs could have had meanings that were quite specific like "a six point buck deer" or quite general "food" in the case of a zoomorph. It is quite likely too that meaning was dependent at least to some extent on the context in which the glyph was found and by its relationship to other glyphs which were nearby. In other contexts, at least in the mind of the maker, the order in which the symbols or their parts were created may have held syntactical significance. It would have been difficult at best to convey that sequence to others once the process was complete. It seems likely too, that just as the meaning of words often changes over time today, that the meaning of petroicons too was modified by the passing of time. Some glyphs probably had layers of meaning or complex nuances. They may have stood for an actual physical object or only an idea or a combination of the two as Chinese ideograms do. Take for instance a zigzag line. Such a line may have indicated a snake, lightening, a water way or trail or a horizon or it may have had more abstract meaning such as crooked, changing, deceiving or variable.

Some simple series of glyphs preserved by markings in stone, initially created to serve as a mnemonic device for shamans preforming a complex set of rituals and incantations, may have eventually evolved into liturgical texts describing the correct ritual procedures for various systems of belief.

CHAPTER SEVEN

CONCLUSIONS

We can realize as this discussion concludes, that understanding the meanings and purposes of rock art is a complex one. Many factors and facets of the task must be recognized and combined if we are to arrive at satisfactory results. Once we have learned to ask the appropriate questions, we can begin to populate our understanding with the appropriate answers and hope that by doing so we can be closer to actually knowing the intent of the original makers of these marks on stone we know as rock art. To the extent this book facilitates that, my marks here will have succeeded.

ABOUT THE AUTHOR

Oregon native and avocational archaeologist D. Russel Micnhimer is a member of the Oregon Archaeological Society from whom he has received numerous Loring and Loring Grants to supplement rock research. He has also given several presentations about his research to that organization. He has had a lifelong interest in prehistory and history and has traveled extensively exploring ancient civilizations, notably in Mexico and South America. For the last two decades he has traveled throughout the Western United States exploring ruins, rock art and other evidence of pre-contact habitation. Micnhimer is co-author with LeeAnn Johnston of *Where to See Rock Art Washington Oregon Idaho* and has written numerous rock art articles for Oregon Archaeological Society publications.   His and Johnston's extensive photographic record of rock art visits are exhibited on his Internet site,   http://www.oregonrockart.com and featured on the prestigious Bradshaw Foundation site http://www.bradshawfoundation.com/oregon/index.php .

ORDER MORE COPIES OF THIS BOOK

QUANTITY   _____

TIMES $14.95 US EACH
   (40% DISCOUNT 5 OR MORE)   _____

SUBTOTAL   _____

PLUS S&H@

$4.00 US FIRST COPY   _____

$2.00 US EACH ADDITIONAL   _____
   (OUTSIDE US ADD $4.00)

TOTAL ENCLOSED   _____

CHECK OR MONEY ORDER ONLY TO

   RUSSEL MICNHIMER
   P.O. BOX 1653
   PRINEVILLE, OR 97754

SHIPPING INFORMATION (PLEASE PRINT)
(PLEASE ALLOW 6 WEEKS FOR DELIVERY)

NAME _____

ADDRESS _____

CITY _____ST_____ZIP_____
TALKINGEARTH@HOTMAIL.COM   954 494 9984

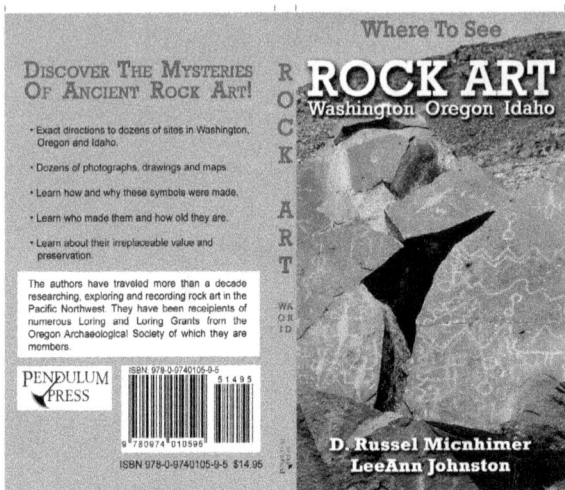

Where To See

DISCOVER THE MYSTERIES
OF ANCIENT ROCK ART!

ROCK ART
Washington Oregon Idaho

* Exact directions to dozens of sites in Washington, Oregon and Idaho.

* Dozens of photographs, drawings and maps.

* Learn how and why these symbols were made.

* Learn who made them and how old they are.

* Learn about their irreplaceable value and preservation.

The authors have traveled more than a decade researching, exploring and recording rock art in the Pacific Northwest. They have been recipients of numerous Loring and Loring Grants from the Oregon Archaeological Society of which they are members.

PENDULUM PRESS

ISBN 978-0-9740105-9-5

ISBN 978-0-9740105-9-5 $14.95

D. Russel Micnhimer
LeeAnn Johnston

Where to See Rock Art Washington Oregon Idaho contains general information about various aspects of rock art and specific information about where rock art can be seen in museums, visitor centers, state parks and public lands in Washington, Oregon and Idaho. Photographs, line drawings and a brief description give readers an idea of what they will find at 39 locations in the three states.

AVAILABLE AT OREGONROCKART.COM

www.ingramcontent.com/pod-product-compliance
Lightning Source LLC
Chambersburg PA
CBHW060903280326
41934CB00007B/1163